The Quality Audit
Handbook

Also available from ASQ Quality Press

After the Quality Audit: Closing the Loop on the Audit Process
J. P. Russell and Terry Regel

Fundamentals of Quality Auditing
B. Scott Parsowith

Quality Audits for Improved Performance, Second Edition
Dennis R. Arter

Quality Management Benchmark Assessment, Second Edition
J. P. Russell

How to Make the Most of Every Audit: An Etiquette Handbook for Auditing
Charles B. Robinson

How to Plan an Audit
ASQ Quality Audit Technical Committee;
Charles B. Robinson, editor

To request a complimentary catalog of publications, call 800-248-1946.

The Quality Audit Handbook

ASQ Quality Audit Division

Writer: Janice L. Smith
for Penworthy Learning Systems

J. P. Russell, editing director

ASQ Quality Press
Milwaukee, Wisconsin

The Quality Audit Handbook
ASQ Quality Audit Division
Writer: Janice L. Smith for Penworthy Learning Systems
J. P. Russell, editing director

Library of Congress Cataloging-in-Publication Data
The quality audit handbook / ASQ Quality Audit Division; writer,
   Janice L. Smith; J. P. Russell, editing director.
        p.   cm.
    Includes bibliographical references and index.
    ISBN 0-87389-374-3 (alk. paper)
      1. Auditing—Handbooks, manuals, etc.   I. Smith, Janice L.
 (Janice Lucke), 1962–   .   II. Russell, J. P. (James P.), 1945–   .
 III. American Society for Quality Control. Quality Audit Division.
 HF5667.035   1997
 657'.45—DC21   96-47516
                                                                          CIP

10 9 8 7 6 5 4

ISBN 0-87389-374-3

Acquisitions Editor: Roger Holloway
Project Editor: Jeanne W. Bohn

ASQ Mission: To facilitate continuous improvement and increase customer satisfaction by
identifying, communicating, and promoting the use of quality principles, concepts, and technologies; and thereby be recognized throughout the world as the leading authority on, and
champion for, quality.

Attention: Schools and Corporations
ASQ Quality Press books, audiotapes, videotapes, and software are available at quantity
discounts with bulk purchases for business, educational, or instructional use. For information,
please contact ASQ Quality Press at 800-248-1946, or write to ASQ Quality Press,
P.O. Box 3005, Milwaukee, WI 53201-3005.

For a free copy of the ASQ Quality Press Publications Catalog, including ASQ membership
information, call 800-248-1946.

Printed in the United States of America

 Printed on acid-free paper

American Society for Quality

Contents

Foreword

The ASQC Quality Audit Division has long sought to adopt or publish a text that explains the commonly accepted quality audit conventions. In our early days as a Technical Committee (circa 1985), we attempted to publish a series of monographs relating to various aspects of quality auditing. We had but one success: *How to Plan an Audit* (Robinson, ed., ASQC Quality Press, 1987). In 1989, Norman C. Frank began the task of developing an outline for what would eventually become this handbook. Upon completion of that outline, Barbara E. Houlihan began the task of gathering material for the various chapters. Responsibility was transferred to John J. Dronkers in 1991. Meanwhile, Educational Testing Services (Princeton, N.J.) was hired to assist us in developing the quality auditor Body of Knowledge. Completion of this Body of Knowledge in 1993 made the need for a handbook even more evident. While there are many fine texts covering quality audit principles, none properly support our Body of Knowledge and the mission of our division. In May 1995, we decided to commit some serious money to the development of this handbook. You are holding the result of our division's commitment and many volunteer hours from our members.

This is our first effort, and we already know there will be a second edition. Even as this book is being printed, our Body of Knowledge is undergoing formal revision. Additionally, there is a major effort underway to update the international quality auditing standard, ISO 10011. The profession is evolving.

This handbook was developed by our members to meet the needs of our members. Contributions came from respected published books, conference proceedings, individual topical papers from our members, telephone interviews, and critical comments from a team of reviewers spanning many organizations and countries. Our division chose to use the approach of hiring a technical writer from outside our profession to harmonize the many divergent opinions. We also hired a project manager to coordinate the overall effort. This approach allowed us to get the diversity of thought we felt was needed to provide a text that reflected our combined member expertise.

We feel that this publication will be a valuable reference for understanding quality audit principles and conventions. We thank you for purchasing it.

Dennis R. Arter
Vice Chair, Technology
ASQC Quality Audit Division

Notes to the Reader

This handbook supports the quality auditor Body of Knowledge, developed for the ASQC Certified Quality Auditor (CQA) program. The text is aligned with the Body of Knowledge for easy cross referencing. Through use of this handbook, we hope to increase your understanding of our Body of Knowledge.

The Use. The handbook can be used by new auditors to gain an understanding of quality auditing. Experienced auditors will find it to be useful as a reference text. Audit managers and quality managers will use the handbook as a guide for leading their auditing programs.

The handbook will also be used by trainers and educators as source material for teaching the fundamentals of quality auditing. The handbook is not designed as a stand-alone text to prepare for the ASQC Certified Quality Auditor (CQA) exam. As for all ASQC certification activities, you are encouraged to work with your local ASQC section for such preparation. *The Quality Audit Handbook,* when used in conjunction with other published materials, is appropriate for refresher courses, and we hope that trainers will use it in that manner.

The Contents. The handbook is organized to be in alignment with the quality auditor Body of Knowledge. We have included this Body of Knowledge in the handbook as an appendix. It is also included in the ASQC CQA brochure (Item B0020). Many concepts and practices of quality auditing are still evolving; therefore, the Body of Knowledge will change over time. As change occurs, the handbook may be out of alignment until it is revised.

One exception to alignment of the handbook and the Body of Knowledge is the placement of auditing terms and definitions. The reviewers and editors felt is was more appropriate to move the auditing terms and definitions from Part 1 to a glossary at the end of the Handbook. In fact, there are two parts of the glossary that contain terms and definitions. The first part is based on the worldwide accepted definitions in ANSI/ISO/ASQC A8402. The second glossary contains the terms as defined in the ASQC CQA brochure. The terms were not combined into one glossary in order to maintain the integrity of the sources of the definitions. The ANSI/ISO/ASQC A8402 definitions have undergone extensive peer review and are accepted worldwide. The ASQC CQA brochure definitions are officially associated with the CQA program but have not undergone extensive peer review.

The Quality Audit Handbook represents generally accepted quality audit practices for both internal and external applications. As such, it may not depict the best practice for all situations. We specifically caution against its use for registration or regulatory auditing.

The handbook uses generic terms to support broad principles. For clarity, specific industry examples and stories from CQAs are sometimes used to explain a topic in the Body of Knowledge. The stories are depicted as sidebars throughout the text, as a means to share experiences of other quality auditors. Industry examples are incorporated with the text. They are not intended to be all-inclusive or representative of all industries. Needless to say, this work cannot address the most appropriate practice for every industry or organization.

This publication, which describes audit methods and their application, is not intended to be used as a national or international standard. Although it references many existing standards, it was not developed under the totally open, consensus process.

Who Wrote It. A broad spectrum of organizations in the United States and around the world is represented by the Certified Quality Auditors who supplied information for the Handbook. About 70 individuals contributed material. A number of published texts were also used to create and develop *The Quality Audit Handbook*. It represents internal and external audits in a variety of product and service industries, regulated and nonregulated.

To avoid the perception of bias toward any particular approach, we chose a unique way to develop the handbook. A professional writer from outside the quality field conducted telephone interviews to supplement the information provided in contributed papers and published texts. Significant issues relating to the principles and intent of quality auditing were referred to a Tie-Breaker Committee for resolution. Extensive peer review further strengthened the manuscript.

Why the Handbook. The ASQC Quality Audit Division sponsored the development of this handbook to promote the use of quality auditing as a management tool—our primary mission. We believe that the Quality Audit Division's 15,000 members possess the greatest concentration of theoretical and practical quality auditing knowledge in the world. In *The Quality Audit Handbook*, we tried to give you the benefits of this collective expertise.

ASQC Quality Audit Division

Acknowledgments

Many members of the ASQC Quality Audit Division contributed to *The Quality Audit Handbook*. Some wrote topical papers specifically for use in the handbook. Others presented technical papers at our annual Quality Audit Conference. Still others participated in telephone interviews. We had members who paid for the privilege of reviewing the draft manuscripts. Finally, we had a Tie-Breaker Committee for the really hard areas. This was truly a team effort.

The order of the acknowledgments is in chronological order of involvement in the project by team and does not reflect the significance of individual contributions.

Early Project Participation (Our Visionaries)
Norman C. Frank
Barbara Houlihan
John C. Dronkers

Topical Paper Contributions
Early in the development of the handbook, division members provided new or existing papers for consideration for the proposed handbook. Some were not selected because they simply did not fit our needs. Putting together a creditable paper is very difficult. We wish to thank all those that prepared and submitted papers to support the

development of the handbook. Here are the authors whose papers were eventually used.

Glena G. Anger and coauthors Robert Cofer, Tom Feyerabend, Joyce Ford, Marti Levy, Patti McGuire, and Betty Wims
Shyam Banik
Rudolph C. Hirzel
Kathryn E. Jackson and Thomas B. Tucker
Joseph H. Maday Jr.
Larry McArthur
Jerry Nation

Writer Organization
Dorinda Clippinger (owner of Penworthy, Inc. of Cincinnati, Ohio) and Janice L. Smith (writer) worked well with the members of the Quality Audit Division. Their professional approach and can-do attitude made the development of the handbook run smoothly. They provided us with a great product.

Interviews with the Writer
Some of the necessary material was not initially available. Additionally, some of the material from the referenced texts was conflicting. We therefore found it necessary to query some of our members by telephone about certain topics within the quality audit Body of Knowledge. They provided supplemental information and examples for us to use. They also helped to fill in the missing pieces of information needed to complete the work.

Dennis R. Arter, PE, FASQC, ASQC CQA
John Barrett, ASQC CQA, ASQC CRE, RAB QS-A
Don Beckwith, ASQC CQA, Ball State University CTC
Mary Carter Berrios, ASQC CQA, ASQC CQE, ASQC CQM
Cheryl A. Boyce, ASQC CQA and RAB QS-LA
John J. Boyle, ASQC CQA
Bruce H. Campbell, PE, FASQC, ASQC CQA, ASQC CQE
Mike Coughlin, ASQC CQA, ASQC CQE
Traci V.A. Edwards, ASQC CQA, ASQC CQE, ASQC CQM
Norman C. Frank, PE, ASQC CQA, ASQC CQE

Marvin C. Gabalski, ASQC CQA, ASQC CQE, ASQC CRE, RAB QS-LA
David A. Kelly, Ph.D., ASQC CQA, ASQC CQE, RAB QS-LA
Judith Ann Malsbury, ASQC CQA, ASQC CQE, ASQC CQM
George Mouradian, PE, FASQC, ASQC CQA, ASQC CQE, ASQC CRE
Robert J. Nash, Ph.D., ASQC CQA, ASQC CQM
Terry Regel, ASQC CQA, ASQC CQE, RAB QS-LA, IRCA LA
Charles Robinson, FASQC, ASQC CQA, RAB QS-LA
Haakon Rud, DnV Certified Lead Auditor
Douglas Stimson, ASQC CQE, RAB QS-LA
Steven Wilson, ASQC CQA

Manuscript Reviewers

It was the job of the reviewers to review text for technical correctness. The many reviewers provided feedback, ideas for developing the work, and examples for inclusion in the handbook.

United States Reviewers

Ronald L. Ackers, PE, FASQC, ASQC CQA, ASQC CQE, ASQC CRE, ASQC CQM, IIE-CST, RAB QS-LA
Douglas G. Anderson, ASQC CQA
Richard M. Baehr, ASQC CQA, RAB QS-LA
Lon L. Barrett, ASQC CQA
Jimmy Bell, ASQC CQA
Bernie Carpenter, ASQC CQA, ASQC CQM, MSQA
Ariel Castro, ASQC CQA
Robert G. Chadwick, FASQC, ASQC CQA, ASQC CQE, ASQC CMI
Robert G. Chisholm Sr., ASQC CQA, ASQC CQE, ASQC CQT, ASQC CMI, RAB QS-LA, QS-9000 Auditor
Jim Coley, ASQC CQA
Peter R. Corradi, ASQC CQA, ASQC CQE, RAB QS-A
Harold Crotts, ASQC CQA, ASQC CQE, ASQC CMI, AAS, Ind. Eng.
Jeffrey A. Deeds, ASQC CQA
Kathleen L. Eaves, ASQC CQA
Cheryl A. Hadley, ASQC CQA
Rudolph C. Hirzel, ASQC CQA, ASQC CQE, ASQC CQM

David Kildahl, ASQC CQA
Ramesh Konda, ASQC CQA, ASQC CQE
Jim Lamar, ASQC CQA
James (Rusty) Lusk, ASQC CQA, ASQC CQE, ASQC CQM, RAB
    QS-LA
Donald Mason, ASQC CQA
Jerry T. Nation, PE, ASQC CQA, ASQC CQE, ASQC CQM, RAB
    QS-LA
Chris Newcomer, ASQC CQA
Martin F. Patton, ASQC CQA, RAB QS-LA, IRCA LA
Steven L. Pearson, ASQC CQA, RAB QS-LA, AIAG Cert. QS-9000
    LA
David Prins, ASQC CQA, ASQC CMI, ASQC CQT, ASQC CQE,
    ASQC CRE, NAPM-CPM
Terry Regel, ASQC CQA, ASQC CQE, RAB QS-LA, IRCA LA
John Rinaldi, ASQC CQA
Gwen E. Sampson, ASQC CQA
Stephen Sheng, ASQC CQA, RAB QS-LA
Ron Spring, ASQC CQA
David L. Thibault, ASQC CQA, ASQC CQE
Alfred F. Wales, ASQC CQA, ASQC CQE
Stony F. Walker, ASQC CQA

Non–United States Reviewers
Steven Britton, PE, ASQC CQE, ASQC CQA (Canada)
Karson K. K. Chui, ASQC CQA, ASQC CQE (Hong Kong)
Darren S. Kent, ASQC CQA (Canada)
Ian A. MacNab (Canada)
Akhilesh N. Singh, IRCA LA (India)
Peter F. Wright, ASQC CQA, IRCA A, AOQ CQT (Australia)
Jorge Xavier (Brazil)
Roger W. Zigmond, ASQC CQA, ASQC CQE (Canada)

Tie-Breaker Committee

The Tie-Breaker Committee members resolved differences that surfaced from the review process. They provided guidance to the editor and writer. The Tie-Breaker Committee helped to ensure that various views were considered. The also kept the project focused on the quality audit Body of Knowledge.

Norman C. Frank, PE, ASQC CQA, ASQC CQE
Linda Reinhart, ASQC CQA
Gerry Sherman, ASQC CQA, ASQC CQE, ASQC CQM

J. P. Russell, Handbook Project Manager
ASQC Quality Audit Division

Part I

General Knowledge, Conduct, Ethics, and Audit Administration

Chapter 1
General Knowledge

While the exact origin of auditing is unknown, references to it appeared in recorded text in Sumeria more than 3000 years ago. Egyptian pharaohs used "overseers" to supervise the construction of the pyramids, and the Greeks and Romans used "auditors" to monitor the progress of their armies in conquered lands. In medieval times, the king's representative—the auditor—would log the names and quantities of items on a ship to provide assurance that all taxes due on cargo would be properly recorded. So from the very beginning, auditors have been associated with controls and compliance. Gradually, others have come to rely on outsiders to provide assurances to interested parties.[1]

Audits are independent, unbiased, fact-finding exercises that provide information to management. This information identifies opportunities and reduces the risk of decisions made by management. It is management's responsibility to take appropriate actions based on the audit information provided. "The audit is a long-established and well-respected activity in the accounting profession. . . . Because of many similarities in the activities of the accounting and quality fields, quality professionals have adopted the same word 'audit,' complete with some of the same modifiers."[2]

WHAT IS A QUALITY AUDIT?

The ASQC Quality Audit Division defines *audit* as "a planned, independent, and documented assessment to determine whether agreed-upon requirements are being met."[3] A *quality audit* is "a systematic and independent examination and evaluation to determine whether quality activities and related results comply with planned arrangements and whether these arrangements are implemented effectively and are suitable to achieving objectives."[4]

Quality auditing may be thought of as the process of comparing actual conditions with requirements and presenting an evaluation of the results to management. Managers want to know if their plans, methods, and controls are achieving the necessary results; quality auditors provide them with that knowledge.[5]

The quality audit is one management tool for determining the compliance and/or effectiveness of a product, process, or quality system. By examining documentation, implementation, and effectiveness, quality auditing is used to evaluate, confirm, or verify activities related to quality. "The quality audit may be a single occurrence or a repetitive activity, depending on the purpose and the results of both the audit and the product/service, process, or quality system concerned."[6] A properly conducted quality audit is a positive and constructive process. It helps prevent problems in the organization being audited by identifying the activities apt to create problems. Problems generally arise through the inefficiency or inadequacy of the concerned activity.

Quality auditing is an overview function that ensures that all functions of an organization having any affect on quality are adequate and are performing as designed. Quality audit results are reported to management and are used to make managerial decisions concerning potential corrective actions.

Quality assurance and quality control are two aspects of quality management. *Quality assurance* consists of "all the planned and systematic activities implemented within the quality system, and demonstrated as needed, to provide adequate confidence that an entity [item] will fulfill requirements for quality."[7] The confidence provided by quality management is twofold: internally to management, and externally to customers or others. While some quality assurance and quality control activities are interrelated, *quality control* is defined as "operational techniques and activities that are used to fulfill requirements for quality."[8] Quality assurance relates to how a process is performed or how a product is made. Quality control, on the other hand, is more the inspection aspect of quality management. Products, processes, and various other results can be inspected to make sure the final object coming off a production line, or the service being provided, is correct and meets specifications.

"A quality audit is not an alternative to an inspection operation. . . . The quality auditor may use inspection techniques as an evaluation tool . . . but the quality audit should not be involved in carrying out any verification activities leading to the actual acceptance or rejection of a product or service. A quality audit should be involved with the evaluation of the process and controls covering the production and verification activities."[9]

Quality audits in their current form emerged shortly after World War II and gained momentum when the military began issuing standards and specifications for products. Quality auditing originally resembled an inspection activity and developed primarily in large manufacturing industries, such as the electronics field, and in high-risk fields, such as the nuclear and aerospace industries.

"All companies and enterprises, regardless of size, can benefit by examining their activities and management systems. This applies no less to local government, civil service, commerce and the service industries than it does to manufacturing industries."[10]

Participants in the Audit Process

A quality audit involves three key participants who may be linked in a number of ways. Described by function, these participants are the client, the auditor, and the auditee.

The *client* is the person or organization who has requested that an audit be conducted. The client usually is senior management requesting an audit of an organizational unit under its jurisdiction, requesting an audit of independent suppliers, or applying for third-party registration.[11]

The *auditor* is the person(s) who plans and conducts an audit. The auditing organization is the unit or function that carries out audits through its employees (auditors). This organization may be a department or function of the auditee; a client; or an independent third party, such as the auditing group of a quality program registrar.

The *auditee* is the organization to be audited and may be a division of the client's organization or an entirely separate entity, such as a supplier. At times, and often in internal audits, the client and auditee are the same person or department.

Internal vs. External Audits

An audit may be classified as internal or external depending on the interrelationships that exist among the participants. Internal audits are first-party audits, while external audits can be either second- or third-party audits. Figure 1.1 illustrates the classifications commonly used to differentiate between types of internal and external quality audits.

First-Party Audit. A first-party audit is performed within an organization to measure its strengths and weaknesses against its own procedures or methods and/or external standards adopted by the auditee organization (voluntary) or imposed on the auditee organization (mandatory). A first-party audit is an internal audit conducted by auditors who are employed by the organization being audited, but who have no vested interest in the audit results of the area being audited. Companies may have a separate audit group consisting of

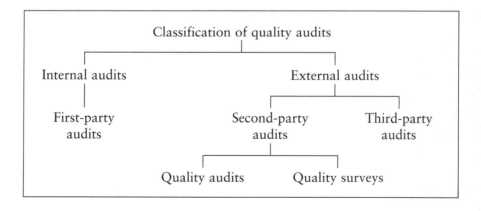

Figure 1.1. Classifications of quality audits.

full-time auditors, or the auditors may be trained employees from other areas of the company who perform audits as needed on a part-time basis in addition to their other duties.

A multisite company's audit of another of its divisions or sub-sidiaries, whether locally, nationally, or internationally, is often considered an internal audit. If the other locations function primarily as suppliers to the main operation or location, audits of those sites would be considered second-party audits, however.

Second-Party Audit. A second-party audit is an external audit performed on a supplier by a customer or by a contracted (consulting) organization on behalf of a customer. A contract is in place and the goods or service are being, or will be, delivered.[12]

A *quality survey,* sometimes called a *quality assessment* or *quality examination,* is a comprehensive evaluation that analyzes such things as facilities, resources, economic stability, technical capability, personnel, production capabilities, and past performance, as well as the entire quality system. In general, a survey is performed prior to the award of a contract to a prospective supplier to ensure that the proper capabilities and quality system are in place.[13]

> **SIDEBAR**
>
> I (an auditor) know of one case in which an organization actually went out to give a supplier an award for the perfect product they had been receiving. However, during the award process it was discovered that the supplier had absolutely no quality system whatsoever in place! The supplier was able to ship acceptable product simply because its employees were good sorters.

Third-Party Audit. A third-party audit is performed on a supplier or regulated entity by an external participant other than a customer. The organization to be audited—or in some cases, the client—compensates an independent party to perform an audit. Third-party audits are performed on behalf of an auditee's potential customers, who either cannot afford to survey or audit external organizations themselves or who consider a third-party audit to be a more cost-effective alternative. Third-party audits are conducted for recognition or registration purposes, not for the purpose of business negotiations. For example, government representatives perform mandatory audits on regulated industries, such as nuclear power stations, airlines, and medical device manufacturers, to provide assurances of safety to the public.

Recognition Purposes. For example, companies applying for the United States' Malcolm Baldrige National Quality Award, which recognizes world-class companies and establishes the criteria necessary to compete internationally, must submit to an examination. More than 35 states in the United States have programs modeled after the Baldrige Award program, and some municipalities present similar awards. Japan's Deming Prize is another example of such an award. The United States and Japan are not unique, because many countries around the globe have established similar criteria.

Registration Purposes. Certain companies wanting to do business in Europe must have their management system registered by audit to one of the ISO 9000 series requirement criteria. Contractors to federal agencies are recognized as registered suppliers by auditing against federal (national) standards.

Customers throughout the world are increasingly demanding that their subcontractors (suppliers) conform to ISO 9000 criteria. The U.S. Federal Acquisition Regulations (FARs) currently state that government contractors that comply with the ISO 9000 requirement standards are not required to comply with other quality standards. In fact, many federal (national) standards have been canceled, and users have been referred to the U.S.-adopted ISO 9000 requirement standards. A third-party audit normally results in the issuance of a certificate stating that the auditee complies with the requirements of a pertinent standard or regulation.

Third-party audits for ISO 9000 quality system registration are performed by organizations that have been evaluated and accredited by a recognized accreditation board (the Registrar Accreditation Board—RAB—in the United States) as being competent to perform audits of companies desiring to achieve quality system registration. A list of registered companies is maintained for selection by potential customers. The registration of companies that supply high-risk regulated products is a government requirement, while the registration of other companies becomes a customer-driven requirement.

The essential service provided by an auditing organization is to verify that the registered company has developed and implemented a quality management system that meets established requirements.

TYPES OF QUALITY AUDITS

Quality auditing originated from product auditing, but has expanded into various aspects of the process and system.[14] Quality audits normally fall into one of three categories: product, process, or system.

Product Quality Audit

A *product quality audit* is an in-depth examination of a particular product (hardware, processed material, or software) to evaluate whether it conforms to product specifications, performance standards, and customer requirements. If an audit is being performed on a service instead of a product, then it is called a *service quality audit*. "Such an audit examines all elements of the product/service and the related quality system elements to evaluate the system against the referenced standards or specifications for that product or service."[15] Elements examined may include packaging, shipment preparation and protection, users' instructions, product performance, and other customer requirements.

Product audits are conducted when a product is in a completed stage of production and has passed the final inspection. The product auditor uses inspection techniques, but the overall aspect of decision is very different. The auditor evaluates the entire product and all aspects of the product characteristics. The product audit has broader scope than an inspection and focuses on whether the observations/findings are isolated or general, if the auditee's resolution should prevent recurrence, and whether opportunities for improvements exist.[16] The sporadic product audit is not a substitute for the normal process output approval (acceptance) procedures.

In contrast, inspection is a part of the product approval process and is conducted on a regular or constant basis. Inspectors check products to verify conformance to standards as stipulated by limited characteristics of the product. Each inspection has a decision rule covering what to accept and what to reject. Inspection usually entails a sampling plan and ongoing sampling, such as examining one out of every five units down the assembly line, while the sample size during a product audit may be very small and on a spot-check basis.

In summary, a product quality audit is the examination or test of a product that has been previously accepted or rejected for the characteristics being audited. Such an audit is a reinspection or retest of the product to measure the effectiveness of the system for product acceptance. It includes performing operational tests to the same requirements used by manufacturing, using the same production test procedure, methods, and equipment. The product quality audit verifies conformance to specified standards of workmanship and performance. This audit can also provide a measure of the quality of the product going to the customer. The product quality audit frequently includes an evaluation of packaging; examination for cosmetics; and a check for proper documentation and accessories such as proper tags, stamps, shipment preparation, and protection.

Process Quality Audit

The *process quality audit* is performed to verify that processes are working within established limits. It examines an activity to verify that the inputs, actions, and outputs are in accordance with defined requirements. A process quality audit covers only a portion of the total system and usually takes much less time than a system audit. The boundary of a process audit should be a single process, such as marking, stamping, cooking, coating, setting up, starting up, or installing. A process audit is very focused and usually involves only one auditor or work crew.[17]

A process audit is a verification by evaluation of an operation or method (regarding a product or service) against documented instructions and standards, to measure conformance to these standards and the effectiveness of the instructions. Such an audit is a check of conformance of process, personnel, and equipment to defined requirements such as time, temperature, pressure, composition, amperage, component mixture, and so on. It may involve special processes such as heat treating, soldering, plating, encapsulation, welding, and nondestructive examination. A process audit checks the adequacy and effectiveness of the process controls over the equipment and operators as established by procedures, work instructions, and process specifications.[18]

Quality System Audit

A *quality system audit* is "a documented activity performed to verify, by examination and evaluations of objective evidence, that applicable elements of the quality system are appropriate and have been developed, documented, and effectively implemented in accordance and in conjunction with specified requirements."[19]

A quality system audit evaluates an existing quality program to determine its conformance to company policies, contract commitments, and regulatory requirements. It includes the preparation of formal plans and checklists on the basis of established requirements, evaluation of the implementation of detailed activities within the quality program, and formal requests for corrective action, where necessary.[20]

Criteria contained in the American Society of Mechanical Engineers (ASME) codes, nuclear regulations, Good Manufacturing Practices, or ISO standards, for example, may describe a quality system. Normally these descriptions state *what* must be done, but do not specify *how* it must be done. The *how* is left up to the organization being audited. An auditor looks at the management systems that control all activities starting with an order coming into a company—how that order is handled, processed, and passed on to operations, then what operations does in response to that order—through delivery of the goods, sometimes including transportation to the site.

A system audit looks at everything within the quality system: the processes; the products; the services; supporting groups such as purchasing, customer service, design engineering, and order entry; and training. It encompasses all of the systems of the facility that assist in providing an acceptable product or service.

WHAT DO AUDITS MEASURE?

Regardless of whether a product, process, or system audit is being performed, quality audits evaluate the adequacy of the documentation; compliance to the documented procedures; and the effectiveness of the procedures and their implementation to accomplish the intended objectives, as applicable. Once the type of audit and the scope of it (with regard to adequacy, compliance, and effectiveness) have been determined, the auditor needs to determine the audit method to be used. Auditing methods are discussed in Part III of this handbook.

Compliance/Conformance

Compliance refers to the "affirmative indication or judgment that the supplier of a product or service has met the requirements of the relevant specifications, contract, or regulation."[21] In contrast, *conformance* is the "affirmative indication or judgment that a product or service has met the requirements of the relevant specifications, contract, or regulation."[22] In common practice the terms are used interchangeably and the term *conformance* is also used to indicate that the process and system have met requirements. ANSI/ISO/ASQC A8402 simply defines the word *conformity* as "fulfillment of a specified requirement."[23]

Compliance looks for strict adherence to a set of rules, which may include requirements, standards, or other needs. The audit is not the arena for questioning these rules; they are set and identified for the audit. Examples of audits involving compliance include regulatory and high risk.

- *Regulatory.* Certain activities of society are regulated by government. Among these regulated activities are production of energy, stewardship of the environment, production of food, protection of workers, and use of medical products. Auditors verify that the applicable laws and regulations in these areas are being implemented to ensure the health and safety of consumers.

- *High risk.* For some events, the consequences of failure are unacceptable. These events include the launching of aircraft, submarines, and space rockets. A complete and thorough audit of the finished product is necessary before it is activated or placed into service. The audit checks inspection records, craft qualification records, design review records, and other forms of proof.[24]

Adequacy and Effectiveness

In addition to establishing conformance with a set of rules, quality audits may measure the adequacy of procedures and the effectiveness of implementation to which those rules assist in achieving basic goals. These goals are usually related to the continuous improvement of the organization.

The principles of quality auditing apply to any type of management assessment. No valid reason exists for separating management auditing into subcomponents. Management has control of resources. The goals of quality, safety, environmental stewardship, and efficiency are all driven by the same set of rules: Define requirements, produce to those requirements, monitor achievement of those requirements, and continuously improve on those requirements.[25]

HOW ARE AUDIT RESULTS MEASURED?

An auditor measures compliance with and conformance to specified requirements by gathering and analyzing *objective evidence,* "information which can be proved true, based on facts obtained through observation, measurement, test, or other means."[26]

Objective evidence is observed or documented evidence that is uninfluenced by prejudice, emotion, or bias. Objective evidence is anything that can prove or disprove whether required activities are taking place. Records, witnessing an event, and discussions with (interviewing or questioning) personnel could all be considered examples of objective evidence. Two auditors examining the same objective evidence should be able to reach the same conclusion.

An auditee presents objective evidence to an auditor to prove that the audited system works as the auditee has explained it and that written documentation exists to support the system. If something cannot be observed, then it needs to be recorded—in the form of a report, a check sheet that confirms that the auditee went through a particular setup, or minutes from a meeting. If an auditor talks to a supervisor and gets one "story," then talks to several operators independently and hears the same explanations, that auditor has built support or evidence for the investigation.

Evidence should be collected on all matters related to the audit objectives and work scope: procedures or work instructions and proof of their implementation, examination of personnel training and qualification records, examination of process controls and records, and reexamination of selected work. Evidence needed to support the auditor's findings may be physical, testimonial, documentary, and/or analytical. Objective evidence may be obtained in several ways: internally from the organization under audit, externally from third parties, or by comparing evidence obtained from two or more sources. Evidence obtained from independent, external sources is more reliable than information obtained from internal sources. Knowledge obtained through physical examination, observation, computation, and inspection is more reliable than interview comments. Evidence derived from records is likewise more reliable than oral evidence. Any evidence should be sufficient, competent, relevant, and useful to be a sound basis for audit findings and recommendations. A rational relationship should exist between the cost of obtaining evidence and the usefulness of the evidence.[27] For example, the costs involved with shutting down a manufacturing plant to obtain data or traveling to 100 service centers to verify that employees know the quality policy may not be justifiable.

Objective evidence can be qualitative or quantitative.

Qualitative Audit Methods

Qualitative methods are used during an audit to collect qualitative data. Qualitative data indicate that a certain step has been conducted. Qualitative audit methods are employed to a greater extent during a quality system audit because the auditor is trying to understand the entire system—the standards and requirements, as well as assessing whether the person being interviewed understands and has implemented the system under examination. Normally in quality systems, information is documented—for example, with records, procedures, drawings, work instructions, manuals, training records, or electronic data on a computer screen or disk.

Objective evidence can be obtained through interview techniques by asking good, open-ended questions. Through interviewing, an auditor can determine not only that has a system been documented and implemented, but that the worker has been trained in its use, is familiar with it, and knows how to use it from a practical standpoint. An auditor can ask for records or say "show me." If a worker says that one out of every 10 units coming down the assembly line is checked, the next logical question is "Do you have a procedure that tells you to check one out of every 10 units?" By presenting the written procedure, the worker confirms that a procedure does indeed exist and that employees are aware of it. However, the interviewing method by itself generally does not provide objective evidence to determine that a system has been documented and/or implemented. A review of documents is needed to verify that a system has been documented; a review of documentation and/or observation of items and/or activities is needed to verify that a system has been implemented.

Quantitative Audit Methods
The dictionary defines *quantitative* in terms of relating to, or expressing in terms of quantity, or involving the measurement of quantity or amount. Quantitative audit methods are used to collect quantitative data. Quantitative data means that a measurement has been taken or that a count has been performed. Quantitative audit methods include sampling. An auditor can use statistically based sampling plans to determine the number of samples to pull for the desired confidence level. An auditor can also count, for example, the number of shipments, number of defects, or number of products approved. Quantitative audit methods are employed most often in product or process audits.

WHY PERFORM A QUALITY AUDIT?

The performance of a quality audit provides management with unbiased facts that can be used to achieve the following:

- Provide input for management decisions (so that quality problems and costs can be prevented or rectified).
- Inform management of actual or potential risks.

- Identify areas of opportunity.
- Assess personnel training effectiveness and equipment capability.
- Provide visible management support of the quality program.
- Verify compliance to regulations.

"The tasks of management include (1) identifying possible sources of problems, (2) planning preventive action to forestall problems, and (3) solving problems, should they arise. . . . Most problems are quality problems related to the quality of work being performed, the quality of items being received, the quality of information being communicated, the quality of available equipment, the quality of decisions made . . . Since all quality problems have a cost associated with them, avoiding, preventing, and solving these problems prevents and reduces unnecessary costs."[28]

The benefits that a quality audit provides vary depending on whether the audit is a first-, second-, or third-party audit. For example, possible benefits of a first-party audit include the early detection of a problem (which gives management the opportunity to investigate and identify root causes, take immediate corrective actions, and ultimately prevent problems from happening again) and the assurance that adequate procedures are established and utilized.

Second-party audits benefit the supplier as well as the customer because they help to eliminate the shipping of nonconformities and to reduce costs and waste. This in turn builds confidence between the supplier and customer, promotes a better understanding of customer expectations, and provides an avenue for quality technology transfer between the customer and supplier. Second-party audits also help ensure a better final product (output) by verifying that there are appropriate controls for inputs into the system.

Finally, third-party audits are performed to meet regulatory requirements or to achieve registration. While achieving registration itself should not be a primary goal of the auditee, the benefits of being registered include provision of added assurance to customers, increased competitiveness, reduced market barriers, and decreased costs of multicustomer audits. "The usual purposes of quality audits are to provide independent assurance of the following conditions:

- Plans for attaining quality are such that, if followed, the intended quality will, in fact, be attained.

- Products are fit for use and safe for the user.

- Laws and regulations are being followed.

- There is conformance to specifications.

- Procedures are adequate and are being followed.

- The data system provides accurate and adequate information on quality to all concerned.

- Deficiencies are identified and corrective action is taken.

- Opportunities for improvement are identified and the appropriate personnel alerted."[29]

"Quality audits are carried out to determine either or both of the following:

1. Suitability of the quality program (documentation) with respect to a predetermined reference standard

2. Conformity of the operations within the quality system to the documented quality program."[30]

CHANGES AND TRENDS IN AUDITING PRACTICES

Although quality auditing in its modern form has been in existence since the late 1940s or early 1950s, the quality audits of today bear little resemblance to those of that period. Ideally, quality auditing in the 1990s is a management tool for improvement and not an activity that management fears or resents.

No one knows for certain what changes will occur in the quality auditing field in the next decade. However, trends in several innovative areas suggest an exciting and enriching future for the profession. Changes in the formation of audit groups, through joint audits or round-robin consortiums, will ensure greater auditor independence and result in a cross-fertilization of ideas among industries. New standards, such as the ISO 14000 series, are being created to address societal and global needs. Also, as companies incorporate a total quality management approach, which emphasizes continuous improvement, the focus of auditing is expected to shift from compliance to effectiveness. Finally, advances in communications technology and the increase in the internationalization of businesses will lead to many changes in the next decade.

Formation of Joint Audit Teams and Round-Robin Consortiums

Joint auditing is a recent trend, especially in regulated industries. Rather than having several separate audit programs for environmental, financial, and safety, auditors join together to perform one audit.

In round-robin consortiums, groups of companies with similar interests each contribute one or two auditors to a group. Then a company desiring to be audited requests that the consortium provide auditors to conduct an audit. The round-robin approach is an excellent way for a company to get independent audits performed; the auditors benefit in turn by gaining auditing experience. Such an audit team must be handled in the same way as a third-party registrar: Confidentiality agreements may have to be signed, and auditors should not audit a competitor or supplier. So the makeup of the audit team must be carefully contemplated. An auditee does not pay for a round-robin audit, unlike third-party registration audits. Since each organization is auditing the others, the cost of contributing the time of an auditor is involved; but the cost is absorbed by all companies that contribute an auditor or use the service.

This concept originated because companies had difficulties getting experienced auditors. The companies involved in a round-robin consortium do not have to belong to the same industry; for example, a textile manufacturer and a metals manufacturer may have auditors belonging to the same team. As a result, a synergy or cross-fertilization of ideas from different industries occurs across the boundary from one industry to another industry.

Round-robin consortiums provide many benefits. Two such benefits are that a company gets an independent audit, and the auditors get the training and experience necessary for some types of certification. These consortiums are an excellent method of getting people qualified and getting an independent audit performed so that a company may know beforehand how it might fare in a third-party audit.

Creation of New Standards

In the early days of quality auditing, very few national or international standards existed to audit against. Some regulated industries (the military, aviation, processed food, and aerospace industries) had national or industry-wide standards, but most other organizations audited against self-determined, self-developed standards or requirements.

In the past 20 years, the development of numerous international, national, and industry-specific quality standards has supplemented internal (self-determined) standards and provided a common reference. The international standards in the ISO 9000 series, first issued in 1987 and revised in 1994, describe *what* elements quality systems should encompass but do not state *how* organizations should implement these elements. Since the management system of an organization is influenced by the objectives of the organization, by its products, and by the practices specific to the organization, quality systems also vary from one organization to another. All international standards in the ISO 9000 series are independent of any specific economic sector. Collectively they provide guidance for quality management and general requirements for quality assurance.

In August 1994, the Big Three Automotive Task Force (Chrysler, Ford, and General Motors) published QS-9000, a set of requirements for automotive industry suppliers. The Automotive Industry Action Group distributes the QS-9000 requirements. QS-9000 is identical to the ISO 9000 series, with additional industry requirements geared specifically toward automotive quality improvement programs. However, while ISO 9001, ISO 9002, and ISO 9003 are strictly compliance-type documents, the addition of a TQM philosophy to QS-9000 moves the resulting document in the direction of continuous improvement. In addition, the International Automotive Sector Group, or IASG, has also published interpretations of QS-9000 requirements. While the QS-9000 document is criticized by some as too restrictive, it is considered by many to be a breakthrough and a forerunner of things to come.

Technical standard guidelines have also been developed to help support quality system standards, such as ISO 10011, *Guidelines for Auditing Quality Systems.*

Shifting Focus

In the 1970s, the primary purpose of auditing was compliance. Auditing in certain highly regulated fields, such as the nuclear industry, is likely to remain compliance-oriented. Quality auditing is, however, expected to focus more on adequacy or effectiveness as it becomes more performance based.

An emphasis on continuous improvement is expected to evolve in the field of auditing. Rather than focusing just on adherence or compliance to a certain standard, companies are assessing their operations against those of world leaders such as in the concept of benchmarking or through comparison to criteria such as that for the Malcolm Baldrige National Quality Award.

As companies are trying to achieve continuous improvement and reach world-class levels, they focus not just on complying with a particular standard, but rather ask, "How far can we reach, what are our goals to get there, and how do we go about that process?" As a result, a large percentage of the applications handed out for the Baldrige Award each year are used for self-assessments within a company and are never used to apply for the award. The comprehensive criteria, which can be used either for self-assessment or for award recognition, are based on how a system needs to be structured to attain total customer satisfaction. Benchmarking, one of the tools used during that process, is defined by the American Productivity and Quality Center as "the process of identifying, understanding, and adapting outstanding practices and processes from organizations anywhere in the world to help your organization improve its performance."[31] Winners of the Baldrige Award are required to share with other companies what they have learned from the process—resulting in an open invitation for others to come in and learn from them.

Advanced Communications Technology

Auditors need to stay current with changes in technology as more and more companies are using electronic media for databases and for document control.

Quality auditing is a service that requires considerable communication, so auditors should be familiar with and consider using the appropriate communication technologies, such as electronic mail, fax modems, digital cameras, notebook computers, cellular phones, and videoconferencing.

With the growing popularity and increased affordability of computers, auditors are constantly searching for new technologies that make quality audits more effective and efficient. Computer technology can reduce audit cycle time, conserve paper, and improve audit effectiveness. For example, electronic mail and fax modems can be used to eliminate the longer turnaround times or higher costs associated with conventional or express mailings. Digital cameras, a technology still in its infancy, are expected to become a valuable tool for auditors. A digital camera takes pictures on a disk; this disk can then be inserted into a computer to show pictures of problems uncovered during an audit. These pictures can be displayed at the closing meeting or can be printed and included in the audit report.

An auditor can use a notebook computer in conjunction with the appropriate software during the audit preparation stage to customize checklists or to create flowcharts. During the audit performance stage, computers can be used to consolidate observations during the audit team's daily meetings and to prepare the preliminary (draft) audit report. A computer also can be used to create (and send via electronic mail, if agreeable to the client) the final audit report. Additionally, if the audit is being scored, spreadsheet programs can format the check sheets and automatically compute the audit scores. In addition to saving time, this scoring method helps to ensure consistent and accurate results.[32]

Cellular phones may be useful when an auditor needs to contact a client or audit manager quickly. An auditor may also prefer to bring a cellular phone when auditing a large or remote facility where a telephone may not be accessed easily. Cellular phones can also increase productivity for people who spend large amounts of time in cars or at airports.

Videoconferencing is used routinely by some auditing organizations. It is a valuable method for bringing groups of people face-to-face without incurring travel expenses. In the future, videoconferencing may prove to be especially important in auditing by eliminating pre-audit visits and follow-up audits in many situations.

The use of electronic media requires other issues be addressed such as security, confidentiality (especially for networks), and document controls (viewing, changing documents, changing code, and backing up data).

Internationalization of Businesses

As auditing has become increasingly global, many auditors are finding the ability to speak a second language to be essential. If necessary, an interpreter (translator) should be employed to facilitate an audit. Additionally, an auditor should be aware of any cultural differences that could affect relationships with the auditee. By becoming acquainted with local customs, an auditor can prevent serious misunderstandings from interfering with the audit process.

SIDEBAR

While performing an audit of a supplier in Japan, I worked late one evening, as was often my custom at home. When I opened the door to exit the office that had been provided for my use, I noticed that all employees of the company were still at their workstations. The Japanese culture apparently dictated that every employee remain until I had left for the night. I was very embarrassed that my conduct had detained so many people unnecessarily. Needless to say, I left promptly at 5:00 the following evening.

CONTINUING EDUCATION RESOURCES FOR AUDITORS

As the field of quality auditing evolves, auditors must strive to keep abreast of changes and trends. Quality auditors must embrace current technology. Those who do not will gradually become liabilities rather than assets. Quality professionals must be committed to increasing their knowledge and improving their skills through continuing education. Continuing education resources include reading (technical literature, case studies, research papers, etc.), attending seminars and classes, participating in professional organizations, and consulting with peers.[33]

Organizations offering assistance to quality auditors interested in furthering their knowledge include the following:

ASQC   The Institute of Internal Auditors, Inc.
611 East Wisconsin Avenue   249 Maitland Avenue
P.O. Box 3005   Alamonte Springs, FL 32701
Milwaukee, WI 53201

Many continuing education opportunities are available through ASQC. Annually, the ASQC Quality Audit Division offers tutorials to reflect current events and trends in auditing and holds an annual Quality Audit Conference to expand auditors' knowledge in quality and related fields. Many other organizations offer correspondence courses in standards and quality management. To obtain continuing education units one must attend conferences or take formal courses.

ASQC requires an auditor who has passed the CQA examination and been certified by ASQC to recertify every three years by (1) retaking and passing an examination or by (2) earning recertification units (points). An auditor must collect a specified number of points in a three-year period to remain certified. Points can be accumulated by attending regular ASQC section meetings, completing additional course work, being employed in the field, writing about topics included in the body of knowledge, and attending or leading seminars or training sessions. This requirement encourages auditors to remain in touch with the audit curriculum and maintain a professional level of expertise. Some companies have additional training and qualification requirements (beyond CQA requirements) for members of their internal audit functions.

Many opportunities exist to learn about the technical aspects of quality. Private consultants teach auditing courses and do on-site auditor training; more and more colleges are teaching statistical process control courses, and courses related to auditing may be part of the curriculum at some technical schools.

Auditors may benefit from staying abreast of technology outside of the field of auditing, as specified in the Certified Quality Auditor's Body of Knowledge. For example, courses in leadership, facilitation and presentation skills, public speaking techniques, time management techniques, and computer training all enhance auditors' performance and help them become more professional.

Auditors are better qualified and better trained than ever before. Continuing education opportunities for auditors, once scarce or unheard of, are abundant and diverse. As the twenty-first century approaches, management can expect to reap the benefits of properly performed audits by exceptionally well-trained personnel.

Auditing is not a stagnant process. It is a continuous learning experience to stay current with product processes, to conform to changes in general auditing standards, and to meet the ever-changing needs of management.[34]

Chapter 2
Professional Conduct and Ethics

Ethics are basic philosophical conclusions about what conduct is right and wrong. As in many aspects of business, it is imperative that quality auditors recognize the importance of ethics in auditing so that they can behave appropriately while carrying out their responsibilities.

ETHICS IN AUDITING

Audit ethics is perhaps the area that demands the most skill from an auditor. Training is available for enhancing skills in checklist development, interviewing techniques, audit documentation, follow-up methods, and almost all other phases of an audit. Very little information, on the other hand, is available on the topic of audit ethics. An auditor's use of questionable or unethical methods during or following an audit can quickly erase the favorable results of an audit and be detrimental to the auditor and the auditing department or organization as a whole.[1]

What Is a Code of Ethics?
An auditor's ethical and moral principles should be compatible with a formal set of ethical standards. ASQC's code of ethics[2] for members is shown in Figure 2.1.

To uphold and advance the honor and dignity of the profession, and in keeping with high standards of ethical conduct, I acknowledge that I:

Fundamental Principles

I. Will be honest and impartial; will serve with devotion my employer, my clients, and the public.

II. Will strive to increase the competence and prestige of the profession.

III. Will use my knowledge and skill for the advancement of human welfare and in promoting the safety and reliability of products for public use.

IV. Will earnestly endeavor to aid the work of the Society.

Relations With the Public

1.1 Will do whatever I can to promote the reliability and safety of all products that come within my jurisdiction.

1.2 Will endeavor to extend public knowledge of the work of the Society and its members that relates to the public welfare.

1.3 Will be dignified and modest in explaining my work and merit.

1.4 Will preface any public statements that I may issue by clearly indicating on whose behalf they are made.

Relations With Employers and Clients

2.1 Will act in professional matters as a faithful agent or trustee for each employer or client.

2.2 Will inform each client or employer of any business connections, interests, or affiliations that might influence my judgment or impair the equitable character of my services.

2.3 Will indicate to my employer or client the adverse consequences to be expected if my professional judgment is overruled.

2.4 Will not disclose information concerning the business affairs or technical processes of any present or former employer or client without his or her consent.

2.5 Will not accept compensation from more than one party for the same service without the consent of all parties. If employed, I will engage in supplementary employment of consulting practice only with the consent of my employer.

Figure 2.1. ASQC code of ethics.

Relations With Peers

3.1 Will take care that credit for the work of others is given to those to whom it is due.

3.2 Will endeavor to aid the professional development and advancement of those in my employ or under my supervision.

3.3 Will not compete unfairly with others; will extend my friendship and confidence to all associates and those with whom I have business relations.

Figure 2.1. *Continued.*

Why Is a Code of Ethics Necessary?

"A formal code of ethics allows quality auditors to approach audit performance uniformly. A formal code provides a benchmark against which an auditee and client can measure an auditor's activities, establish an auditor's independence, and recognize potential conflicts of interest."[3]

Ethical standards serve as a general guide for auditors. Auditors often rely on personal judgments and past experiences to determine ethical conduct in specific situations, however. Auditors' personalities, temperaments, auditing styles, and basic perceptions can vary tremendously. By incorporating a set of ethical principles into their daily activities, auditors can maintain the high standards of conduct, honor, and character needed to conduct proper and meaningful auditing practices.[4]

With experience, auditors gain knowledge about the audit area, application of the quality system, area processes, and gain insight into various management styles. Auditors who continually display ethical characteristics during the audit process establish reputations for fairness and objectivity—an absolute necessity in the profession.[5]

APPROPRIATE AUDITOR BEHAVIOR

While the *duties* of an auditor are important, the *behavior* of an auditor, especially in areas that involve confidentiality, often has a greater impact on the success of the audit. Furthermore, the auditor's ability to communicate effectively with management sets the tone for the entire audit and greatly influences the outcome.

Standards of Performance

Auditors must comply with high standards of honesty, integrity, work ethic, diligence, loyalty, and commitment.[6] They should be independent, that is, free from bias and influences that could affect objectivity. Also, auditors have a duty to keep confidential certain information obtained during the course of an audit.

The auditee must be confident that the auditor will conduct an audit professionally and that the auditor possesses the integrity and technical knowledge to successfully complete the audit. Auditors are expected to exercise *due care* during the performance of their activities. This concept means that an auditor should be sufficiently competent to arrive at conclusions similar to those that another auditor would reach in the same or similar circumstance. Since an audit only samples a particular product, process, or system at a particular point in time, an auditor cannot be held responsible if an audit fails to recognize all deficiencies or irregularities in a system, as long as that auditor has used theoretically sound sampling techniques, has complied with applicable standards, and has adhered to a code of ethics.[7]

Confidentiality Concerns

Because businesses could suffer great financial loss if customers or competitors were to gain access to processing knowledge and trade secrets, an auditor often is required to sign a confidentiality agreement, or nondisclosure agreement, before an audit begins. Such an agreement, which states that the auditor will not disclose any proprietary information gained during the course of the audit, should be reviewed and approved by the auditing organization's legal council before the auditor signs it. An auditor could accidentally or deliberately nullify such an agreement orally, in writing, or even through body language.

Discussing proprietary information with others destroys the integrity of the audit function. While it is acceptable for an auditor to discuss actual audit experiences with other auditors, the discussion should be generic so that the auditee cannot be identified. Proprietary information should never be divulged in a sharing situation with other auditors.

One technique when auditing in a nondisclosure area is for the auditor to rely on memory only and not write audit notes, since such notes could become accessible to the public and would be discoverable in litigation.

Even body language could disclose proprietary information. For example, when asked a question about a proprietary process, an auditor's shrug or raised eyebrows could signal the answer even if no words were spoken.

An auditor needs to be very flexible to be able to accomplish audit objectives even when the auditee erects barriers. At times, a company may be in the process of getting a patent on a new method, for example, and may flatly refuse to allow the auditor to view a certain portion of that system. In these instances, the auditor must respect the auditee's wishes and "audit around" the undisclosed area. If the inputs going into the undisclosed area appear to be correct and the outputs are likewise acceptable, then the auditor can assume that the undisclosed process is doing its job correctly.

Likewise, a company sometimes will refuse to allow an auditor to look at the procedure for a certain process even though a written procedure is required. To verify that the procedure exists, the auditor can ask the auditee to hold up the procedure and certify that it covers the relevant process. The auditor may never actually view the details, but can assume that a procedure does exist and is approved for use.

Such situations often resolve themselves on subsequent audits involving the same parties. As an auditee becomes more comfortable with the audit team and places greater trust in the ethics of the team members, the need to limit access to certain areas often becomes nonexistent.

Additionally, companies in certain highly sensitive industries, such as those pertaining to national defense, may require that auditors obtain security clearances. This requirement should be specified well in advance of the audit to permit sufficient time for processing the request. Without the proper security clearance, an auditor may be restricted to certain areas of a company.

Language When Communicating with Management

By approaching an auditee in a diplomatic and objective manner, an auditor can set a tone of success for an audit.[8] An auditor must be aware that each auditee views the audit process differently, on the basis of individual management style, culture, personality, and opinions. Many auditees are reluctant to welcome auditors into their world. Resentment, fear, and anxiety are obstacles that must be overcome. By diplomatically presenting and maintaining the audit program, an auditor can influence an auditee's perception of the audit function as well as the overall success of individual audits.[9]

An auditor can establish good rapport with an auditee early in the audit by being respectful, courteous, and appreciative of any special arrangements made for the auditor's comfort and convenience. By demonstrating that the audit has been adequately planned and prepared for, and by making every effort to maintain the audit schedule, an auditor indicates efficiency and a desire to disrupt business as little as possible during the audit.

Maintaining open communication channels throughout an audit is essential. An auditor must listen attentively during interviews, allow the interviewee adequate response time, and refrain from asking leading questions. Frequent and timely communication of findings, questions, and concerns gives both the auditor and the auditee opportunities to request clarifications, address corrective action, examine the scope of the situation, and discuss the progress of the audit.[10]

Additionally, an auditor can set a positive tone for an audit by highlighting commendable findings and observations.

RESPONSIBILITIES OF AN AUDITOR

In addition to the usual responsibilities of an auditor, certain difficult situations require careful handling for successful resolution. Possible conflicts of interest should be recognized and reconciled before an audit begins. The detection of unsafe, unethical, or even illegal practices during an audit may rapidly change the planned course of the audit.

Other less obvious, but equally challenging, situations may include antagonism, coercion, and even time-wasting techniques employed by the auditee to slow down or stop the audit process.

When a Conflict of Interest Exists

If an auditor has any connection with the organization being audited, the auditor must relay this information to management or decline to conduct the audit, whichever seems more appropriate. Conflict-of-interest situations encountered during an external audit include (1) previous employment of the auditor (or close relative) by the auditee or a major competitor of the auditee, regardless of the reason for separation; or (2) holding of significant amounts of stocks or bonds by the auditor in the auditee's business or that of a major competitor.

During internal audits the auditor may face a third conflict-of-interest situation: The auditor may have been involved in the development of the quality system under evaluation. If the auditor developed the process or wrote the procedure, objectivity is difficult to maintain when the process or procedure is audited for suitability against a reference standard. The auditor would not, however, be precluded from evaluating the compliance of the system with the documented quality program.

By avoiding conflicts of interest, an auditor upholds independence. To maintain integrity of the audit function, an auditor should withdraw from the audit or bring in someone else to perform portions of the audit if a conflict of interest exists.

When Unsafe Activities Are Detected

In some industries, an auditor may need to access potentially hazardous areas in a company during the course of an audit. Usually auditors are provided with proper safety equipment, such as goggles or hard hats, and face no physical danger as long as regulations are enforced and the process is functioning properly. Sometimes, however, negligence or inexperience on the part of the auditee's employees, a deficiency or malfunction of equipment or a process, or a combination of these may result in potentially dangerous situations.

When an unsafe practice is detected, whether within or outside the scope of an audit, an auditor must not ignore it. In an internal audit, an auditor should immediately inform the manager so that the problem can be worked up the internal chain until it is resolved. If, for example, an auditor in a supplier's facility sees an unsafe operating process or system that could result in a major accident, cause an explosion, or result in the release of unsafe chemicals, the auditor must document the situation immediately and bring it to the auditee's attention. The audit can be completed in safe areas, otherwise the audit must be stopped and the auditors returned to the safety of their office. In most situations, management welcomes information about liability risks or other potential danger.

When Unethical Activities Are Detected

An auditor finding evidence of wrongdoing, whether within or outside the scope of an audit assignment, has an ethical duty to bring the matter to the attention of management for action. Such matters should be documented and the evidence safeguarded. The auditor must be aware of and apply the ethics of the profession and the law in this regard.[11]

If management "sponsors" allegedly illegal activities, either internally or externally, the auditor's employment may be threatened. An auditor should have access to legal counsel to resolve questionable issues. The U.S. Congress and various states have passed laws protecting people who report incidents of wrongdoing. Referred to as "whistle-blower statutes," these laws protect auditors and others. Questions about specific laws should be directed to the appropriate federal, state, or local government authorities.

An auditor may encounter unethical situations during the course of an audit, such as when an auditee is shipping defective products. The auditor should verify the situation and then inform the audit manager as well as the auditee. If the problem is caused by an oversight, it should be corrected immediately; however, an auditee who knowingly ships defective product may be unwilling to correct the problem. In this case, the auditing organization should refuse to return to that company. If a third-party audit is being performed, the auditor should immediately report the situation to the client. If the auditee is a supplier, the auditing organization may delay or stop the shipments (if given the authority to do so) until the appropriate management function can resolve the issue. The auditing organization may advise its management to cancel any existing contracts and find more reputable sources for the item.

SIDEBAR

> One of the most blatantly unethical activities I have observed as an auditor was by a supplier who knowingly shipped empty outer casings for a particular device. The casings contained a sticker stating, "If this casing is open, your warranty will be invalidated and there will be no refund." After verifying what I was seeing, I discussed the situation with the audit manager, who in turn discussed it with auditee management. We ended up pulling our order from this supplier.

An auditor who detects unethical activities within the auditing organization should inform the manager, who will usually work up the internal command chain until the problem is resolved. If the same or similar situation recurs often, the auditor's principles are probably not compatible with those of the organization and new employment should be considered. Unethical activity that is in violation of internal company policy should be reported directly to management whether it is unethical behavior of another employee or of a supplier. Unethical behavior on the part of an ASQC member that violates the ASQC code of ethics should be reported to the local section of ASQC for investigation and possible reporting to the ASQC Ethics Committee.

Although not commonplace, bribery is another example of an unethical situation that an auditor may encounter. An auditor encountering obvious bribery should flatly refuse the offer and stop the audit. The client and auditing organization management must be alerted and give the matter immediate attention. Gift giving could be a less obvious form of bribery. Many public agencies and private companies have specific regulations and policies on ethical behavior. For example, a limited dollar amount, usually about $25, may be specified for gifts that the auditor may accept ethically. An auditor has an obligation to refuse or return any gift that exceeds the stated amount and has the option of refusing any item. Many auditors will accept an offer of an inexpensive meal since they feel that both parties benefit from the rapport established in a casual setting, while others will refuse even the offer of a soft drink.

> **SIDEBAR**
>
> During the course of an audit, I happened to mention that I was an avid tennis player. Several weeks later I received a case of tennis balls from the auditee. I wrote a polite note and sent it to the auditee, along with the case of tennis balls.

In the international auditing arena, an auditor must be familiar with local customs so that potentially unethical situations can be interpreted correctly and responded to appropriately. For example, in the United States it is considered a breech of ethics for an auditor to accept a gift or favor from a person in the audited organization, but in Japan gift giving is part of the culture and it would be rude for the auditor to decline.[12] As quality auditing becomes increasingly global, organizations and individuals must be aware of such differences to prevent serious cultural misunderstandings from undermining the audit process.

When Other Difficult Situations Arise

At times, an auditor may encounter other difficult situations that are counterproductive to the auditing process. For example, an auditee may be antagonist or coercive. Interviewing may be made ineffective by an interviewee who talks too much or not at all. An auditee may also use time-wasting tactics by deviating from the audit plan. In any difficult situation the auditor should remain polite but firm, maintaining complete control of the audit.

Defusing Antagonistic Situations. Sometimes employees may be openly hostile to an auditor. The reasons for such reactions may be totally unrelated to the audit, or the employees may be reacting to what they feel is a personal attack by the auditor on their abilities to do their work. An employee may have been part of the team that developed a process or a particular system, or may have just gone through a six-month long endeavor to improve something that the auditor is now picking apart. When an auditee "gets defensive," the auditor could perhaps separate people and suggest a quick coffee break to defuse the situation. If the conversation must be continued, do so later when everyone is calm again.

Combating Time-Wasting Techniques. An experienced auditor will immediately recognize most time-wasting tactics employed by an auditee. An auditor needs to lead an audit and not allow the auditee to take control. If an auditee attempts a lengthy presentation at the opening meeting or an extended plant tour, for example, the lead auditor should call a halt to these activities or limit the time spent on them. Often a lead auditor can eliminate wasted time by making specific requests during the audit planning stage. For example, many audit teams prefer a catered lunch to going off-premises for several hours. Of course, auditee management and the client should be notified when an audit team repeatedly encounters delay tactics or if the audit schedule is severely compromised by such delays.

Figure 2.2 lists some common time-wasting ploys and suggests possible solutions that an auditor may use when faced with each problem. An auditor adjusting to specific situations could likely think of equally effective solutions.

Overcoming Language and Literacy Barriers. ANSI/ISO/ASQC Q10011-2-1994 specifies that audit personnel must either (1) be fluent in the agreed language of the audit or (2) have available at all times personnel with the necessary technical language skills.[13] When necessary, an auditing organization should employ a skilled interpreter to assist with an audit.

Even when all primary participants in an audit speak the same language, the auditor may at times encounter language or literacy barriers when attempting to interview individual employees. These same barriers may prevent the employee from understanding and/or performing described tasks. A written procedure may solve the problem; but if the employees are unable to read or understand the procedure,

The Problem	One Solution
Requested personnel are unavailable to the audit team.	Auditor could politely state that absence of key personnel may prolong the audit or that the audit's scope may have to be modified.
Escort is repeatedly late in the mornings.	Auditor could suggest that the audit may have to continue for an extra day.
Auditee makes the auditor wait repeatedly for needed supplies or requested documentation.	Auditor should request needed supplies during the audit planning stage and anticipate documentation needs in advance.
Constant distractors occur during interviews (area is noisy, constant phone ringing, or other interruptions).	Auditor could suggest that they move away from area or close doors if possible; phones should be set to call forwarding or answered by someone else.
Interviewees state that they were not informed of the audit and are not prepared.	Auditor should confirm that employees are aware that an audit is taking place and ask auditee management about the state of readiness of the quality system to be audited.

Figure 2.2. Common time-wasting ploys and possible solutions.

then the problem has not been addressed. If an auditor understands the physical process before going into an audit and then focuses on the work, some of the literacy issues may be overcome with the aid of flowcharts and other simple diagrams. At times, an auditor may need to ask extremely simple questions to overcome a lack of language skills.

Avoiding Other Problems. Selecting an auditor from within an organization (for a first-party audit) can cause problems, especially in the case of a one-site operation. The objectivity of an auditor working in an area of previous employment may be questioned. Often former peers may be intimidated, uncooperative, or use the auditor as a sounding board for complaints, making it difficult for the auditor to obtain objective information. They also may think that the auditor will not report procedural violations. Furthermore, the auditor's knowledge of how a product, process, or system functions may be outdated, and time may be wasted as the auditor follows wrong paths using incorrect criteria.

Ideally, an auditor will not be assigned in an area of previous employment. For internal audits, though, such assignments cannot always be avoided. The negative effects must be weighed against the benefits that selecting an auditor from within the organization may offer. Such benefits may include a superior understanding of the organization's product or service and the processes involved in its production, and a strong familiarity with the applicable quality requirements or standards.[14]

Auditors performing external audits must abide by certain rules to avoid possible ethical conflicts. Besides looking and acting professionally at all times, other responsibilities of an auditor in external audits include maintaining the confidence of the auditing organization by never divulging proprietary information to the auditee, refraining from speaking negatively about the auditing organization or previous auditees, and refraining from discussing the performance of previous auditees with people in the organization currently being audited.[15]

Whether facing one of the problems mentioned or more difficult situations, an auditor must remain focused and in control of the audit function.

Chapter 3
Audit Administration

An *audit program* is "the organizational structure, commitment, and documented methods used to plan and perform audits."[1] For an audit program to operate effectively, the objectives of the audit function need to be clearly defined. These objectives should lead to quality system improvements made in a cost-efficient manner. The success of an audit program is often determined by how the program and its auditors are supported and perceived by management and other personnel in the organization. A well-managed audit group not only performs duties related to the planning and performance of an audit, but also strives to standardize and improve its performance so that audit results are meaningful and lead to continuous improvement within the organization.

All management systems, including quality auditing, consist of four fundamental activities: planning, performance, measurement, and improvement. Often referred to as the plan-do-check-act (PDCA) cycle, these activities are basic to any total quality management approach.[2]

PDCA is commonly known as the Shewhart cycle because it was created by Walter A. Shewhart, a pioneer in statistical quality control. In Japan it is known as the Deming cycle after W. Edwards Deming, who first described it to them.[3]

The "plan" stage, or preparation phase, starts with the decision to conduct an audit. It includes all activities from audit team selection to the on-site gathering of information. This audit preparation phase is discussed in Part II of this handbook.

The "do" stage, or performance phase, begins with the on-site opening meeting and includes the gathering of data and analysis of it. Normally, data collection is accomplished by conducting interviews, monitoring activities, and examining documentation and records. It concludes with the closing meeting. The performance phase of auditing is discussed in Part III of this handbook.

The "check" stage, or reporting phase, of the PDCA cycle covers the translation of the audit team's conclusions into a tangible product. It includes publication of the formal audit report.

The "act" stage, or closure phase, of the PDCA cycle is associated with reactions to the report and the recording of the entire effort. For audits resulting in the identification of weakness, the closure phase includes tracking and evaluating the follow-up action taken by others to fix the problem and prevents recurrence. Often this part of the closure phase is referred to as *corrective action*.[4] The reporting and closure phases of auditing are discussed in Part IV of this handbook.

OBJECTIVES OF AN AUDIT PROGRAM

An auditing organization's first step in successfully implementing an audit program is to define the objectives of the audit program. While objectives vary from one organization to another, they often include statements such as the following:

- To perform and present audits meaningfully (in terms that appeal to management interests)
- To ensure that all required audits are performed regularly, with audits of critical functions performed more frequently
- To ensure that only trained, qualified, and independent auditors are employed to perform audits
- To promote a strong alliance between the audit function and the auditee
- To standardize the auditing process and form a basis against which to measure continuous improvement
- To support the objective/strategies/goals of the organization

If they meet management's needs, audits can be valuable tools for evaluating a company's performance. However, the benefits realized from the performance of an audit must always be weighed against the cost of performing the audit. "Such costs include the auditor's time spent preparing, performing, following up and completing an audit; the auditee's time spent participating in and following up the audit results; and overhead costs associated with an audit."[5]

ENHANCING CREDIBILITY OF THE AUDIT FUNCTION

For an audit to be meaningful, it must be deemed credible. An audit must be performed by competent individuals who gather and handle all information pertaining to the audit in an unbiased and ethical manner. To ensure independence, an audit group should be structured so that it does not report directly to the manager of the function being audited. Additionally, management must support the audit function and use the audit results in an appropriate manner to establish and maintain the credibility of the program.

Auditors' Qualifications

Using knowledgeable, experienced, skilled, capable, and well-trained auditors is the most effective way to enhance the credibility of the audit function. Becoming an ASQC Certified Quality Auditor is one way for an auditor to demonstrate competence. The use of unqualified auditors who possess little knowledge or who do not have the ability to assist management in making good decisions or improving a process can discredit the entire audit process.

SIDEBAR

> I am familiar with the attitude of one company in choosing members for its internal audit group. Rather than selecting its best employees and training them as auditors, this company uses the audit group as a means of relieving its worst employees from their normal duties. These people are exactly the wrong ones to be in that position.

A good auditor does not have to be an expert in the area being audited, but does need to be knowledgeable in the discipline of quality auditing and have an understanding of what is being observed. At times, an auditor must be able to grasp that understanding in minutes or ask another member of the audit team to verify an observation or to assist in other ways.

Auditors need to be able to communicate effectively, both orally and in writing. Since a large part of the job consists of interviewing, a good auditor must ask intelligent, proper questions and listen attentively. Interviewing techniques are discussed in Part III of this handbook.

An auditor needs to be tactful and offer feedback in a positive, nonintimidating manner. An auditor needs to be especially considerate of an auditee's employees. The audit process is disruptive to daily operations and can cause inconvenience for employees. By sticking to the proposed audit schedule and not retaining employees through their coffee or lunch breaks, the auditor shows sensitivity to those being audited. If people see the audit process as a nuisance, they are less likely to cooperate, and the auditor risks being unable to complete the assignment well or on time.

SIDEBAR

As an auditee, I had received an audit agenda for a third-party audit. The first item on the agenda was a quick plant tour. However, as we started the tour, the auditor requested to see a certain area of the plant that was not scheduled to be looked at during that audit. As we were leaving the area he said, "I know it's not on the agenda, but I would like to ask a couple of questions here. It won't take long; I don't want to get off schedule, but I'd like to start here." A day and a half later the auditor was still in that area asking questions. He never audited another department in the entire facility.

An auditor can enhance the credibility of the audit function by avoiding conflict-of-interest situations and ethical conflicts. An auditor must have the ability to look at information objectively and handle confidential information ethically. An auditee must trust an auditor not to divulge proprietary information to competitors or to others who can use it to their benefit. Even internally, audit results usually are not shared between locations, especially when the locations report to different management.

Management's Support

An audit program is an extension of the management function. An audit should identify with systems and not with people. Thus, it must be supported by senior management and should be perceived positively by the rest of the organization. When management emphasizes the importance of the audit function and its usefulness to the organization, such an attitude permeates the entire organization. If management fears or resents the intrusion of the auditing function, this attitude will likewise infiltrate the organization. When an audit program has been set up to collect worthwhile information that managers can use to improve the company, the benefits are twofold: An improved market position may result, and the people who are ultimately going to be audited can realize the benefits of the audit process.

Management's response to audit results is also important. If the obtained data are used to improve a system and its management, employees can see the benefits derived from an audit. This fact is especially true in an internal audit program, which helps a company identify its own weaknesses before customers or others do.

On the other hand, if an auditor or management focuses on the people being audited rather than on the processes or systems, the value of the audit program can rapidly decline. It is not necessarily one individual's fault when there are many audit findings or when a system is not implemented well. Such problems may be primarily caused by the way the system is structured. Therefore, a company needs to focus its efforts on improving the system.

While auditing a company that I had visited many times in the past, I was struck by the coldness and unwillingness to cooperate of many of the employees. I had found these same employees to be very friendly and cooperative during prior audits. Finally, someone confided to me that the results of the previous audit that I had performed had been used as a basis for employees' performance appraisals. Although I tried to discuss the situation with the manager of that area, he insisted that performance appraisal was a proper use of audit results.

Note: One auditor's reaction to this dilemma was to state in the audit report that corrective action needed to be taken to eliminate the practice of using audit results in employee performance appraisals. In another case, the auditor declined future audit assignments in that particular department.

MANAGING AN AUDIT PROGRAM

Auditing is often a function of an organization's quality department, although in some organizations it can reside in the manufacturing, operations, compliance, or technology department. Regardless of where the auditing function resides, it must be (1) independent of the areas to be audited, (2) supported by management, and (3) deployed in a positive manner.

Management of the audit function includes the following activities.

- Establishing a reporting relationship for audit function
- Establishing audit authority, operational freedom, constraints, and boundaries
- Ensuring the availability of adequate resources for all audits
- Determining the use of a single auditor or audit team
- Staffing and training auditors
- Establishing procedures, processes, and criteria for an effective and efficient audit program

- Establishing methods for evaluating an audit program
- Establishing audit schedules
- Confirming audit dates and any requested changes of audit dates
- Setting priorities for audit subjects
- Reviewing audit performance
- Providing periodic reports to management on the status of the quality audit program

An *audit manager* or *audit coordinator* is responsible for preparing an audit schedule, budgeting resources, and assisting with or overseeing other administrative duties related to the auditing function. Additionally, the audit manager staffs and trains the audit department and must subsequently monitor and evaluate auditors in the performance of their duties.

Scheduling and Budgeting for Audit Assignments

When scheduling an audit, an audit manager typically identifies the client and the client's requirements and obtains information about the auditee. The audit manager also selects the audit team (often with recommendations from the lead auditor) and identifies other resources needed, such as a technical specialist or consultant.

In internal auditing, an annual audit program plan that should be updated as changes occur is recommended to prevent scheduling difficulties. The auditee facility should have a copy of the plan a year in advance, showing the week that an audit will occur at the site.

A *horizontal audit* is an audit of one system (such as training) across several departments. A *vertical audit* is an audit of several systems (such as testing, test equipment, test status, and nonconformances) within one department.

Staffing the Organization and Monitoring Performance

A group responsible for performing audits should have a documented, formalized program that includes selecting, training, and monitoring the performance of all auditors.[6]

Larger companies normally have a separate audit group consisting of a few professionals to perform internal audits. This group reports to either an audit manager or to the quality manager. Smaller companies may have an ISO coordinator who recruits and trains employees to perform audits part-time in addition to their regular assignments. This arrangement ensures the availability of well-qualified, technically competent people who know the audit system and who can perform internal audits.

Team play is vital in auditing, since a customer expects all auditors from an organization to follow unified policies and perform similarly. Discussion of unusual situations, findings, or problems encountered during an audit enables an entire team to benefit from the experience and gain new skills and insights. Such discussions enhance team spirit within a department, encourage open communication, and promote uniformity of auditing practices. Some auditing departments schedule weekly meetings to accomplish this growth, and may even maintain minutes of the meetings for future reference. All such discussions must remain within the department—discussion outside these confines is unethical and compromises a department's integrity.[7]

Evaluating the Audit Program

All audit programs and audit teams must be periodically evaluated. An internal audit program can be evaluated through management reviews in which management appoints an independent audit team to review audit results to get some insight on the types of audits that are being done. In the case of a multisite company, auditors from another location may be asked to come in annually to audit the audit team. This evaluation could include watching the audit team perform an audit; examining auditor training records and audit schedules; or looking at sample audit results, corrective actions, and follow-up activities to see if the program is working as intended. For external audits, an auditee may be asked to fill out a sheet rating audit team members' interviewing skills and interaction with personnel, and indicating the auditee's satisfaction with the audit report.

Part II

Audit Preparation

Chapter 4
Audit Plan Preparation and Documentation

The preparation stage of an audit begins with the decision to conduct an audit. For a third-party audit, or when an outside organization is being used to conduct a second-party audit, the client selects and contracts with an auditing organization. For a second-party audit, the employer of the auditing organization usually initiates the audit by request or by approval of an audit schedule. The client and/or the employer of the auditing organization defines the purpose and scope of the audit, as well as the standard against which the audit is to be conducted. The auditing organization, in return, prepares the audit plan and other working papers, selects the audit team, and notifies the auditee in writing of the impending audit. For a contracted second-party audit, the client should notify the auditee.

For an internal audit, the preparation stage may be less formal. Since internal audits often are scheduled on a regular or continuous basis, such as quarterly, an interoffice memo may suffice for notification. Also, the lead auditor and manager of the area to be audited are likely to have greater contact during the audit planning stage.

An auditing organization must prepare carefully for an audit. A well-planned audit is more likely than an unplanned or poorly planned audit to progress according to schedule, earn the auditor the respect and the full cooperation of the auditee, and efficiently utilize the time and other resources of both auditee and auditor.

When preparing to be audited, an auditee organization has certain responsibilities: ensuring that the audit team will have adequate working space and that necessary personnel will be made available as needed. The auditee often assigns an escort to the audit team to function as a liaison with employees, management, and the audit team.

If preparation for an audit has been inadequate, the audit team risks wasting time during the performance stage of the audit or performing a mechanical audit on the basis of a "canned" checklist. An unprepared auditor may focus on trivial matters or "pet peeves," or spend more time in a conference room than in the work areas. Such an audit is of little value to anyone, since it fails to assess the quality system and wastes time and money.

Nine preparation steps should be followed from the time the auditor receives an assignment to the time the audit starts.

1. Define the purpose of the audit.

2. Define the scope of the audit.

3. Determine the audit resources to be used.

4. Identify the authority for the audit.

5. Identify the performance standards to be used.

6. Develop a technical understanding of the processes to be audited.

7. Contact the persons to be audited.

8. Evaluate lower-tier documents to higher-level requirements.

9. Write checklists of the data needs.[1]

AN AUDIT PLAN

Upon receiving an audit assignment from a client, an audit manager usually assigns the duties for a particular audit to a lead auditor, who will be responsible for all phases of that audit. The lead auditor is responsible for preparing an *audit plan*, generally a one- to two-page document that serves as a link between audit planning and audit execution. An audit plan identifies the following items.

• The tentative date and place of the audit

• The auditee and organizational units to be audited

- The audit team members
- The scope and purpose of the audit
- The standard being audited against (specific sections of the standard may be included)
- The expected duration of the audit
- The expected date of issue of the audit report

In addition, when applicable, the audit plan may list confidentiality requirements, transportation requirements, or required health and safety permits or security clearances.

During the audit preparation phase, the auditing organization must define the audit's purpose and scope (with information from the client) and identify the needed resources and applicable reference standard. Based on these criteria, the audit team is selected and the authority for the audit is verified. The lead auditor then secures the appropriate documentation, prepares—or ensures that other members of the audit team prepare—the applicable checklists and other working papers, and determines the proper data collection methods. The written audit plan should be approved by the audit manager or the client and/or by the auditee.

DEFINING AN AUDIT'S PURPOSE

A client normally provides an auditing organization with a purpose statement for an audit. Usually this statement is specific; however, a client may state the purpose in general terms with the understanding that the auditor will refine it before stating it in the audit plan. In the case of a continuous audit—that is, an audit performed on a regular basis—the purpose may have been defined and known by all parties well in advance of the audit.

Since first-party audits are performed to assure management that goals and strategies of an organization are being met and that the audited area is in compliance with particular quality standards, the purpose normally involves improving existing operations. Several sample purpose statements for first-party audits follow.

The purpose of this [first-party] audit is

- To assure continued implementation of the management system, to evaluate the effectiveness of the system in meeting the stated goals and objectives, and to identify opportunities for continuous improvement in product, process, and system

- To review the mechanical assembly area's compliance with procedures and to evaluate the procedures for opportunities for improvement

- To confirm that project engineering, document control, and procurement activities, being performed in support of basic design, are being accomplished in accordance with the quality assurance manual, selected integrated execution procedures, and governing project procedures, including, as appropriate, client requirements

- To assess the progress of the quality system toward meeting the requirements of ISO 9001:1994 as outlined in the current quality manual.

For a second-party audit, an auditor's quality assurance department or the purchasing department normally determines the purpose of the audit and communicates it to the auditee. The primary purpose of a second-party audit is to assess a supplier to verify that contract requirements are being followed or to assess a potential supplier's capability of meeting specific requirements for a product or service. By determining that the supplier is meeting the requirements specified in a contract, the purchaser gains confidence in the quality of goods and services being delivered.[2] Examples of purpose statements for second-party audits follow.

The purpose of this [second-party] audit is

- To assess the capability of XYZ Company to meet contract requirements by a review of the available resources and by obtaining objective evidence of management's commitment to the quality requirements of our product

- To verify that the materials, equipment, and work being performed under contract 12345-P-001 are in accordance with the procurement documents, as specified in section 6 of this contract, and that the work is being executed by qualified personnel

- To identify the possible cause of recent nonconformities by conducting a comprehensive assessment of the tasks, procedures, and system documentation—including records—related to the production of the wireless widget

Most third-party audits are performed by auditing organizations to determine the compliance of the auditee's systems with agreed-upon criteria. In the case of an audit for registration, an auditor examines an auditee's systems for compliance with a specific standard; for example, ISO 9001 or current Good Manufacturing Practices. The purpose statement for most third-party audits is very specific. Typical purpose statements for third-party audits follow.

The purpose of this [third-party] audit is

- To establish relative compliance to the requirements of ISO 9001 for the purposes of registration of the company's quality system

- To assess the compliance of the quality system to all requirements of ISO 9001:1994 for the purpose of recommending the organization for registration to the standard

- To assess the compliance of the organization to all requirements of regulation 123 for the purpose of recommending approval or disapproval as a supplier

The client determines and states the purpose for an audit, but the audit team will often add detail to the purpose and scope statements. By looking at the specific circumstances surrounding an audit and by examining the auditee's audit history, an auditor can confirm that required corrective actions have been implemented and make judgments about which areas might require less attention. Areas that involve less risk and areas with excellent audit histories may require less sampling.

ESTABLISHING AN AUDIT'S SCOPE

The scope of an audit is developed in conjunction with the purpose statement. While the purpose states the reason for the audit, the scope establishes the boundaries by identifying the exact items, groups, and activities to be examined.

The auditor and the client must agree on the scope; it is documented and communicated in the audit plan to confirm a common understanding.

Examples of scope statements for first-, second-, and third-party audits follow.

> **First-party:** To audit the purchasing manual for wireless widget production
>
> **Second-party:** To audit the heat treatment facility as it relates to contract number 95-003
>
> **Third-party:** To audit the design and manufacture of gaskets, seals, and other compounded elastomer products for commercial and automotive applications at Plant Number 1, 123 Main St., Anytown, USA

Defining the scope of an audit helps to maximize the use of limited audit resources. Determining the scope of an audit also keeps an auditor focused and keeps the audit from becoming a "witch hunt" or "fishing expedition." An auditor should not seek to uncover problems in areas outside of the audit's stated scope, although such problems may emerge in the course of some audits. In such case, the auditor must be prepared to address those concerns. For example, an auditor should investigate when overdue calibration of equipment is observed, even though that equipment might not pertain to the process being audited or fall within the audit scope.

Using Audit Resources Effectively

Achievement of audit objectives depends largely on the availability of sufficient resources: personnel, money, and time. Not only the client and auditor carry resource obligations; the auditee is also held to commit adequate resources to the audit. Planning ensures resource availability, as well as its proper use.[3]

The scope of an audit significantly affects resources and time requirements. If the scope is immense, a large audit team will be needed to complete the audit in a reasonable time frame. If the scope is too large for the available resources, the audit may have to be scheduled for a time when adequate resources will be available, or the scope may have to be narrowed. However, too narrow a scope wastes valuable resources. Clarifying the scope makes audit planning and execution efficient, since the availability of resources directly bears on the achievement of audit objectives.

Observing Problems Outside of the Stated Scope

While auditors should remain within the scope stated in the audit plan, they may discover problems beyond that scope. An auditor's reaction to such a discovery may depend on the severity of the problem, its impact on the quality system, and the type of audit being performed. For example, an unsafe practice or one with serious legal ramifications cannot be ignored, while a minor process problem may not be acknowledged in the formal audit report. However, a minor problem should be communicated to the auditee.

In internal audits, where management's goal is to improve the quality system, problems that interfere with that goal usually are not ignored since continuous improvement of the quality system cannot be promoted if an auditor intentionally overlooks obvious problems. Therefore, the audit team may expand the stated scope and look into the problem. Internally, since the purpose of an audit is to provide an objective view of an operation to assure upper management that the system works as planned, the system is effectively implemented only if corrective action can take place if and where it is needed. In an internal audit, problems need to be identified so that appropriate corrective action can take place.

Conditions outside the scope of the audit should not be included in the formal report as a finding, or violation, for that particular audit. Conditions should be reported directly to the client and the auditee if a serious condition adverse to quality exists or if a possibility of litigation exists. However, minor process problems need only be reported to the auditee.

Sometimes an auditee will want to expand the scope of an audit. Expanding the scope is permissible before an audit as long as the team has time to prepare for the modified scope. If an auditee asks to have the scope expanded once the performance stage has begun, the lead auditor should suggest that the next audit encompass the additional area, since the team will not have done the necessary preparation or may not have adequate time to investigate thoroughly.

Chapter 5
Audit Team Selection Criteria

Once an audit's purpose and scope are confirmed, an audit team must be assembled. Often a lead auditor has already been selected and has completed some of the planning activities. The lead auditor usually participates in the selection of audit team members and may help determine the desired size and composition of the audit team. Each member of the audit team must be independent of the functions being audited.

ACCOUNTABILITY OF AN AUDIT TEAM

An audit team is responsible to the client, the person or organization that hired (directed) them to perform the audit.

An audit team is also accountable to the auditee, because its goal is to help the auditee improve; that is, to assess the organization or process so that the auditee knows what is working and where opportunities for improvement exist.

Finally, members of an audit team are accountable to the audit manager or registrar for whom they are working. The actions of audit team members reflect upon the auditing organization and therefore must uphold the standards set by it.

SIZE OF AN AUDIT TEAM

When selecting an audit team, the auditing organization must determine the number of auditors needed to complete the job. Often the scope of an audit, the time frame in which it is to be completed, and any budgetary concerns will determine whether a single auditor or an audit team is needed to complete the job. The multiple auditor, or audit team, approach allows depth of inquiry and breadth of examination. In addition, it encourages balance since no single individual can possess all of the technical knowledge and personality traits necessary in all audit situations. However, the audit team approach should be used only when the scope of an audit warrants the labor expense. One well-trained and experienced auditor may be all that is required to conduct a meaningful and effective audit.[1]

An audit team may break down into mini-teams to perform portions of an audit. Each mini-team consists of two persons—one to interview personnel, and another to listen and take notes during the interviews. Seldom does the availability of personnel permit such a luxury, except when members of an audit team are accompanied by auditors-in-training.

When scheduling for an audit, the lead auditor should calculate the estimated number of personnel-hours needed to complete each portion of the audit to determine the total number of team-hours required for the audit. For example, if the sum of personnel-hours is 10, then one auditor should be able to complete the audit in 10 hours; two auditors working as a team but at different areas simultaneously should theoretically complete the same audit in five hours. The lead auditor ensures that the size of the audit team is appropriate on the basis of the amount of work to be performed and its complexity, the availability of personnel and other resources, and the desired time frame in which the audit is to be completed. Additionally, the lead auditor should consider the physical size and layout of the space in which the auditors will be working.

A simple formula for determining the number of auditors suggested by a reviewer is as follows:

A = Average interview time in hours per interviewee

Effort (in hours) = (A × Number of employees × Percentage of employees sampled) + Opening meeting + Closing meeting + Report time + Planning

Number of auditors = Effort/Elapsed or allocated time for the audit

Lead Auditor Selection and Duties

Every audit team has a *lead auditor* or *audit team leader*. When the audit team consists of only one auditor, that auditor is the lead auditor. When more than one auditor is needed for an assignment, the lead auditor—normally an individual with supervisory experience or management capabilities—is usually identified prior to the other team members and participates in their selection.

The lead auditor has ultimate responsibility for the satisfactory performance of all phases of the audit, as well as for the professional conduct of the audit team members. As the representative for the entire audit team, the lead auditor is responsible for initiating and maintaining communication with the auditee. The lead auditor prepares the audit plan, conducts the opening and closing meetings, reviews findings and observations identified by auditors, prepares and submits an audit report, and evaluates corrective action. Other communication may include daily briefings throughout the audit, which are conducted by the lead auditor.

A lead auditor, whose duties include auditing, and directing and monitoring team members, usually has more auditing experience than other team members and is more familiar with the standard being audited against.

Audit Team Selection and Duties

When preparing an audit plan, the lead auditor (and/or client or audit manager) should assess the complexity of the activities to be audited and select team members who possess the qualifications or expertise needed to perform that audit. If the area to be audited is highly specialized, the auditing organization may have to go outside of its own ranks to hire a specialist or consultant who is experienced in that area. To avoid misunderstandings, a specialist must be briefed, prior to an audit, about his or her expected role. Often an audit team is a combination of quality assurance personnel, who are trained and experienced in auditing techniques, and technical specialists, who are trained and experienced in the area to be audited.[2]

Personnel are selected for specific quality auditing assignments on the basis of experience or training that indicates qualifications commensurate with the complexity of the activities to be audited.[3] Each auditor is responsible for preparing suitable working papers for the portion of the audit for which he or she will be responsible. Working papers are discussed in detail in Chapter 9 of this handbook.

The responsibility of an audit team is to gather factual evidence of compliance or noncompliance of the audited area to the standard. Since the audit function intrudes on daily operations, an auditor has a duty to gather information promptly, objectively, and considerately. After comparing and analyzing observations, an audit team should be able to draw conclusions about the system's adequacy and effectiveness, if requested, in relation to the standard and report those findings in a timely manner.

Additionally, audit team members should be free from biases or conflicts of interest, comply with standards of ethical conduct, and exercise due care in the performance of their duties. These concepts are discussed in Chapter 2 of this handbook.

In summary, the number of personnel and the experience and qualifications of the personnel assigned to an audit depend on the amount of material to be covered, the availability of personnel and other audit resources, the amount of time available to perform the audit, and the subject of the audit.[4] A general quality system audit obviously will require different auditor skills than an audit of a chemical processing operation, bank, university, or software company.

EDUCATION AND EXPERTISE OF THE AUDIT TEAM

While a formal post-secondary education and previous work experience are helpful for those desiring to work as quality auditors, auditing is a learned discipline. An auditor's qualifications result from a combination of formal education; training; orientation; experience; continued professional study and work; passing of examinations; good performance record; and acceptance by peers, subordinates, clients, auditees, and employers.[5]

Education and Experience

Quality auditors should have a combination of work experience and education. Quality auditors should be qualified by an authority, for example, ASQC, RAB, or their own organization. One method of proving qualifications is to become an ASQC Certified Quality Auditor (CQA). To become a CQA, an auditor must have experience in one or more of the areas identified in the CQA Body of Knowledge, at least a high school education, and a commitment to ASQC's code of ethics. In the past, auditors usually had a general background in the quality field. Today, many quality auditors have diverse backgrounds and advanced technical degrees or are individuals with service industry degrees in areas such as hotel management.

Training and Recertification

An auditor must have training to ensure competence in auditing skills, related standards and regulations, general structure of quality assurance programs, auditing techniques, and the like. Competence may be developed through orientation on related standards and implementation procedures, training programs on subjects related to auditing, and on-the-job training.[6]

Auditors should maintain their technical competence through continuing education and current relevant auditing experience. ISO 10011-2 suggests training with subsequent examination in standards against which audits are to be performed and auditing techniques. In addition, management skills are required, especially for lead auditors.[7]

Companies should offer an organizationwide certification program for all auditors that includes training and awarding certificates to identify "approved" auditors according to the company's standards. An auditor needs training in conducting audits—training in the standard to be applied, training in objective evidence gathering, and training in interpersonal relations.

Auditors should be trained to write audit observations on the checklists and notes used by audit teams. At least one team member should be familiar with the department operation or scope of activities to be audited. A lead auditor usually has more experience, may be more highly trained in the applicable audit standard, and may have more training in conducting audits. Policies and procedures defining the qualifications for lead auditors often require a certain number of years of experience or a specific number of audits to be performed before promotion to this level.

Recertification of auditors is important and should be required of all auditors. Continuing training—perhaps a three- or four-hour refresher course every two years—coupled with experience in performing audits is a reasonable expectation. Such requirements help an auditor keep up with changes in standards and ensure currency with an organization's policy and procedures in auditing techniques. An audit is intended to be a learning device to help an organization continuously improve its operations, and auditors should likewise strive to continuously improve their performance.

Interpersonal and Other Skills

Regardless of the level of education or training, an auditor who lacks certain interpersonal skills will not be able to conduct an effective audit. Good communication skills, both oral and written, are essential, as are excellent listening skills.

Auditing methods include listening, questioning, evaluating, judging, documenting, planning, and controlling an audit; administering; leading; supervising; and decision making. Interpersonal communication skills such as tact, adaptability, and the ability to analyze evidence and draw conclusions from it are especially important in auditing.[8] An auditor must often criticize other people's work or at least question the validity of someone else's actions, which must be done with a certain degree of tact. Furthermore, an auditor must be able to handle situations where conflict is imminent.

An auditor must be able to understand the technical materials presented during an audit. Depending on the complexity of an audit, the auditor must be able to ask probing questions and get to the root of the problem.

An auditor must be able to present a case clearly and concisely. Auditors do not make assumptions; evidence must be verified. An auditor should be unbiased, never going into an audit looking for something specific (a hidden agenda) and trying to prove it. An auditor also needs to realize how far a team's authority extends, and should not exceed that authority. Most of the necessary interpersonal and other skills needed by auditors are developed through experience and training.

Chapter 6
Sources of Authority for Conducting Audits

As soon as an audit team is selected, it must verify its authority to perform the audit. By specifying the authority for the audit to all involved parties, an auditor confers legitimacy to the audit and removes or minimizes the adverse feelings the auditee may experience when informed of the forthcoming audit. Also, this step keeps the auditor from wasting time preparing for an audit that has not been authorized.[1]

The authority to perform an audit may come from a single source or a combination of sources. The most important thing is not where the authority comes from but that it does indeed exist. Without a specific authority source that permits an audit, an auditor has no right to perform an audit.

AUDIT AUTHORITY

The authority to perform an audit can come from inside or outside the auditee organization. Internally, authority may come from an organization's quality program or from the chain of command. Externally, authority may reside in purchase agreements, industry standards, or government regulations.

Internal Sources
Internal sources for authority are either organizational or hierarchical. The term *organization* describes functions or groups but does not

rank them. The word *hierarchy* refers to status, particularly among individuals. Internal audit authority can come from either source or a combination of them, depending on the company's structure.

Organization. The source of authority for the performance of internal audits usually resides in a document, often called a quality manual, that describes the organization's quality program. This document should define the authority of certain groups or individuals to perform audits.

At other times, a company's quality policy (policy statements about auditing) defines and authorizes audits. If an organization agrees to voluntarily meet certain industry standards, for example, then the quality policy specifies that those standards will be met. In this case, an audit is a planned group of activities to assure management that the organization is meeting those industry standards, which are usually promoted as voluntary, but which may be required or forced upon organizations to be competitive in the industry.

Sometimes an organization decides to adopt or adapt certain criteria even though it is not required to do so. For example, an organization may elect to meet the ISO 9001 or ISO 9004-1 requirements even though it has no intention of applying for registration to ISO 9001. Likewise, the Malcolm Baldrige National Quality Award criteria may be used as a basis for quality improvement even when an organization does not intend to apply for the award.

Hierarchy. Hierarchy is the chain of command that controls how work is delegated and how responsibilities are assigned within an organization. Rather than being driven by written procedures (as for organization authority), an audit is driven by the people who have authority. The audit authority must be higher in the organizational structure than the functions being audited. For example, it would be extremely difficult for a division that is striving for ISO 9001 registration to commission an audit for corporate headquarters, even if headquarters is also striving for registration. Also, at times the vice president of operations, for example, might request a quality audit of department operations. This kind of audit is not defined or required by the organization's policy and procedure, and is usually requested at a higher level. The client would be the senior management person at a facility, or corporate executive management requesting an audit of a certain activity, system, process, or product.

External Sources

At times the authority for an audit is external to the auditee organization, as in the case of authority specified by a contract, standard, or regulatory body.

Contract. The authority to perform external (second-party) audits should reside in the purchasing agreements—a contract or purchase order—between an organization and its suppliers. Sometimes this authority is not readily visible; it may be included under a rights-of-access heading. A rights-of-access clause gives a customer or regulation body the right to inspect or audit a supplier facility and/or product or service. A clause usually specifies reasonable access during normal business hours, for example. Federal Acquisition Regulations require federal government agencies to include this authority in most procurement documents.

A contractual audit source is common in second-party audits. The source of authority is the signed contract between two parties: a supplier and a purchaser. Proprietary processes (for example, research and development projects or processes that are being conducted for a competitor) are defined and are excluded from the concern of the auditor. Access to plant locations is restricted in these circumstances, but should be defined in advance.

Standards. National and international standards are documents such as the ISO 9000 series for quality management. These standards may be followed voluntarily or may be imposed by contract.

Industry standards are written to clarify, amplify, and, in some cases, limit federal regulations. For example, in the pharmaceutical industry, voluntary industry associations such as the Health Industry Manufacturers Association have developed standards that may be used as the basis for internal audits. After an industry has demonstrated the effect of voluntary standards, the best practices may be incorporated with federal regulations. However, industry standards are not regulatory documents.

Regulatory. International, federal, state, or local law may be the source of authority in certain regulated industries. The courts have enforced and reinforced the rights of certain regulatory bodies to conduct inspections and audits of certain organizations to monitor their compliance with the law. Regulatory bodies include organizations that oversee safety, health, and environmental laws.

Chapter 7
Requirements Against Which to Audit

Audits of quality programs require reference standards against which to judge the adequacy of the plans. "The reference standards normally available include:

- Written policies and procedures of the company as they apply to quality

- Stated objectives in the budgets, programs, contracts, etc.

- Customer and company quality specifications

- Pertinent government specifications and handbooks

- Company, industry, and other pertinent quality standards on product, processes, and computer software

- Published guides for conduct of quality audits

- Pertinent quality department instructions

- General literature on auditing[1]

Standards are the norms or criteria against which the performance of an activity is measured. Performance standards come in four levels.

1. Policy documents that cannot be challenged. Examples include corporate policy statements, international and national quality system standards, regulatory standards, and business sector standards.

2. Transition documents. Often called manuals, one should exist for each section, department, or division. Examples include corporate manuals and plant manuals.

3. Procedure documents. These include the step-by-step requirements for doing a job.

4. Detail documents. These documents, such as drawings, purchase orders, product specifications, and inspection plans, explain specific tasks.[2]

"Standards, codes, and regulations . . . are issued by related industrial or professional associations, by national standards writing organizations concerned with the intended marketplace, and by international bodies."[3]

WHY MUST AN AUDIT BASIS EXIST?

To perform an audit, an auditor must be aware of the audit basis, sometimes called reference standards or performance standards, since the compliance or adequacy of a system in regard to certain requirements cannot be measured until those requirements are defined. Regardless of the requirements, an audit must be performed against a basis for reference.

REQUIREMENTS AGAINST WHICH AUDITS ARE PERFORMED

"A client must clearly define the purpose of the audit and the standard of performance against which the auditor's findings will be compared."[4] These reference documents can include quality system, product, or process standards; contracts; specifications; or policies.

Standards

Certain international, national, and industry standards are mandated for many organizations. Audits verify compliance with the applicable standard, whether it be the ISO 9000 series, QS-9000, or the ISO 14000 series. At times, an organization may voluntarily adopt certain standards by incorporating them with contracts or policies even though there is no requirement to do so.

Contracts

In a second-party audit, the purchase order or other contract states the specific requirements that must be met, and an audit is performed to verify that the supplier is meeting those requirements. A contract may include references to a specific standard, such as ISO 9001.

Specifications

Specifications usually refer to product audits. An auditor examines physical dimensions or chemical compositions, for example, to see if they are in compliance with the specified requirements.

Policies

Internally, many companies regularly assess compliance with their own quality policies or policy statements. These policies are often stated in quality manuals and are the basis for the quality program.

Chapter 8

Importance and Utility of Quality Documentation

Before performing an audit, an auditor must secure documentation of the quality policies or practices of a company. Then compliance of a product, process, or system with the requirements specified in the documentation is assessed.

SECURING QUALITY-RELATED DOCUMENTATION

An auditor should contact the auditee to determine the availability of quality-related documentation and to request copies. Proprietary material contained in the documents may be removed before it is sent to an auditor. Naturally, paper has been the conventional form of documentation, but documentation can be in any medium that can be recorded, reviewed, and retrieved. For instance, magnetic media, voice recordings, and videotape are all acceptable forms of quality-related documentation.

A quality auditor verifies, evaluates, and reports compliance by assessing systems, processes, and products against quality-related documentation. Processes are compared to quality objectives and standards, while products are tested and inspected to determine conformance to engineering specifications or standards. Documents that specify quality requirements include the following:

- Quality manuals
- Procedures
- Detail instructions

- Workmanship standards or models
- Policy manuals
- Blueprints and drawings
- Project plans
- Quality plans
- Specifications
- Strategic plans to identify quality objectives
- Certificate of compliance forms
- Industry practices/methods (such as those of the American Society for Testing and Materials)
- Forms used to record data
- Schedules (production, project, or equipment)
- Trade practices
- Service standards
- Software operating manuals
- Work instructions
- Routing cards
- Preventive maintenance plans
- Quality inspection plans
- Purchase order forms

Written procedures are reviewed before an audit starts because the policy drives the audit preparation. In an audit with a scope limited to training in an organization, for example, the appropriate part of the standard that describes the training requirements becomes part of the documentation for that audit, along with the corporate policy concerning training, the records of training for the individuals involved, and the quality plan for training.

USING QUALITY-RELATED DOCUMENTATION

Reasonable documentation is secured before an audit so that the auditor can determine if the system is properly designed. An on-site audit will then determine if the system is functioning. Information contained in documents must be appropriate, adequate, and current if the documentation is to be used in decision making. The quality manual, document master list, or other similar document should instruct the auditor where to locate and how to obtain applicable documents. Reviewing these documents before the audit helps an auditor prepare working papers and determine where to concentrate effort during the performance stage.

Documentation should meet minimum expectations in identifying where all of the organization's requirements are defined and what the policy of the organization is relative to meeting those requirements.

When prior audit information exists it should be reviewed, as part of an auditor's checklist, to ensure that corrective action has been implemented effectively. Sometimes an observation is not a violation, but an emerging trend. During audit preparation, an auditor may examine data to see if this trend has continued or if some action has been taken to reverse it.

An auditor should review past audit records to identify specific areas likely to have continuing or repeat problems and to determine the status of actions taken earlier to resolve any noncompliance. The audit team should verify that the corrective actions implemented following previous audits have remained in effect and that they have prevented the problem or noncompliance from recurring.[1]

Chapter 9
Checklists, Guidelines, and Log Sheets

An audit checklist is the primary tool for giving order to quality audits. With a well-planned and well-defined checklist, success is achievable. Without a checklist, an auditor has a disjointed, disorganized activity and no place to document failed efforts.[1] Before developing the checklists, an auditor must know what the governing requirements documents say.

A completed checklist

- Provides objective evidence that an audit was performed

- Provides order and organization

- Documents that all applicable aspects of the quality program were verified

- Provides historical information on program, systems, or supplier problems

- Provides the essence for the closing meeting and audit report

- Provides an information base for planning future audits[2]

The purpose of a checklist is to gather information during the course of an audit that the auditor will need to justify the audit findings and observations. The checklist serves as a guide to each member of the audit team to ensure that the full scope of the audit is adequately covered. The checklist provides space for recording the facts gathered during the fieldwork, with places to answer yes/no questions and numerous areas for taking notes.

A checklist is a set of notes and specific instructions about specific things and specific areas, specific questions to ask, and specific techniques to use during an audit. Checklists or written procedures are used to assure continuity and comprehensive coverage of the area of interest, and to provide documented evidence of the questions that were reviewed and give the results of the review.[3]

A checklist has space for two kinds of information. One is a standard set of information that every auditor looks for. Some examples follow.

- Does the person being audited have access to written procedures and applicable work instructions?

- Is the procedure up to date?

- Does the scope of this employee's training cover the observed activities?

- Is the organization structure proper for what the employee is expected to do in the observed procedure?

- Are appropriate records being maintained?

The specific format and construction of a checklist may vary from auditor to auditor, depending on what works best for the auditor. Some checklists are yes/no questions that reference a specified requirement, others are open-ended interview questions that test the limits of a procedure, and yet another variation are statements providing additional instruction for the auditor. Variations of the first checklist question may be: Does the person being audited always have access the latest version of the procedure? Verify, through observations, discussions, and review of documents, that individuals have access to written procedures and applicable work instructions covering their activities.

In addition, many checklists contain a set of questions for each section of the requirement standard that is being audited against. This part of the checklist includes questions about management responsibilities, training, quality planning, etc. These "canned" or generic checklist items should be supplemented with time-specific and circumstance-specific questions and observations that the auditor wants to note during that audit.

Deviations from the checklist may result from a change in the audit schedule or an observation that indicates a possible problem. A checklist can be expanded as necessary.[4]

An audit checklist is flexible; audit observations need not be restricted to what the auditor has planned. Also, it is permissible to abandon or make adjustments to some of the checklist items during daily meetings. A checklist is nonlimiting: It does not restrict what an auditor needs to do; it is simply a way to plan so that the auditor knows what to look for and observe in the given area.

Guidelines are additional documented instructions considered good audit practice that may provide additional information for conducting the audit but are not considered mandatory.

Log sheets are another kind of working paper prepared in advance of an audit. A log sheet contains notes and is a record of activities performed during an audit, what the auditor observed, and who the auditor talked to.

Chapter 10

Development of Data Collection Methods

An auditor must develop a plan for collecting specific evidence needed to answer certain checklist questions. The collection plan provides the auditor with space for recording the results of examinations and identifying people who were interviewed. The auditor should ask open-ended questions that result in recording verifiable yes/no data. The questions asked should deal with causal factors—the methods, materials, machinery, labor, measurement, and environment—that may affect a specific action.[1]

Data are observations of fact and can be qualitative or quantitative. Sources of data could include records from the auditee as well as observations that an auditor makes during audit performance, such as counting the number of press cycle openings or observing an operator during a prescribed, defined operation. Qualitative data relate to the nature or attribute of a *single* observation, regardless of frequency. Quantitative data means either that measurements were taken or that a count was made, such as the counting of the number of defective pieces removed (inspected out) or a certain number of cycles of molding press observed during a time period. The number of complaints that a complaint-handling system received during a certain time period is another example of quantitative data.

DETERMINING THE APPROPRIATE DATA COLLECTION METHOD

An auditor, as part of audit planning, will usually have access to work instructions or written procedures. If the system has been well established, the written procedures will describe what records need to be maintained, who maintains the records, who collects the data, and what kind(s) of data are collected. As a result of this preparation, an auditor should know what to expect in terms of data sheets or records when reaching the audit site.

An auditor should have a sampling plan in mind, which should be described on the audit checklist. For example, an auditor will be familiar with the inspection records on a production line and may decide to sample eight of them. In any case, the auditor must ensure that the sample is not biased. See the "Sampling Theory and Procedures" section of Chapter 20 (pages 144–145) for more information on selecting samples.

TRAINING THE AUDITOR IN THE USE OF DATA COLLECTION METHODS

An auditor must be familiar with different data collection methods and their strengths and weaknesses. Proper training teaches auditors which methods can be used, and which ones cannot, for a specific task in particular situations. The audit program can dictate which data collection methods are for compliance and which ones can only be used for inference. An auditor needs to understand basic statistical methods and must be able to choose the method that gives the desired information. Auditors should understand the functions and limitations of different auditing tools and know what is considered appropriate for specific uses. Auditing tools are discussed in Part V of this handbook.

Chapter 11
Audit Plan Communication and Distribution

An audit plan is a written description of the various elements of an upcoming audit. An audit plan is not the same as an audit schedule. The audit plan describes what will be covered in a particular audit or sequence of audits. The audit schedule states what audits will be performed within a certain block of time.[1] Figure 11.1 shows a sample audit plan.

COMMUNICATION OF AN AUDIT PLAN

Before issuing an audit plan, the lead auditor should contact the auditee by phone to verify the proposed date of the audit. After an audit plan has been prepared, the date of the impending audit should be confirmed in writing. For an internal audit, notification is done by memo; for an external audit, it is done by letter. The notification letter or memo should be addressed to the senior person in charge of the area to be audited. For internal audits, this person is probably the department manager or area superintendent. For external audits, this person is usually the plant manager or president.[2] Figure 11.2 shows a sample audit notification letter.

Even when an auditor prepares the letter or memo, the client should sign it. This formal notice should be delivered before the field visit, usually about 30 days in advance. However, notification procedures can

---

Audit Plan—2/22/9X

Audited organization:

ABC Industries, City, State

Purpose:

To verify conformance (compliance) and effectiveness of the quality system using ISO 9002 (ANSI/ISO/ASQC Q9002-1994) quality system standards and to report any nonconformance(s) to ISO 9002 requirements.

Scope of the audit:

The ABC production facility and support activities will be included in the audit. The audit includes all departments that support the production of gizmos that are responsible for meeting ISO 9002 requirements. The areas of interest include the purchasing, quality assurance, laboratory, distribution, order entry, scheduling, production, and training departments.

Requirements:

As specified in ANSI/ISO/ASQC Q9002 and existing ABC company policies and procedures.

Applicable documents:

The quality (policy) manual(s)—QM9002

Unit procedures that cover the ANSI/ISO/ASQC Q9002 requirements

Other regulatory requirements and industry standards

Overall schedule (detailed interview schedule to follow):

March 23, 199X

8:00 A.M.	Orientation for auditors (safety and environment)
9:00 A.M.	Opening meeting (for auditees)
9:30 A.M.	Tour/review documents
10:30 A.M.–4:00 P.M.	Interviews and observations
4:00 P.M.–5:00 P.M.	Audit team meeting

Figure 11.1. Audit plan.

March 24, 199X

      8:00 A.M.–8:30 A.M.   Daily briefing with ABC coordinator

      8:30 A.M.–1:00 P.M.   Interviews and observations continued

      1:00 P.M.–3:00 P.M.   Audit team meeting, prepare report

      3:00 P.M.–4:00 P.M.   Closing meeting

Team members:

  John Doe, Lead Auditor, ASQC CQA

  Jane Doe, ASQC CQA

Approved: _____   Approved: _____
          Audit Organization   ABC Industries

Figure 11.1. *Continued.*

specify a different amount of time—varying from one week to several months.

DISTRIBUTION OF AN AUDIT PLAN

Members of an audit team receive copies of the audit plan, as does the auditee. The auditee is responsible for distributing the audit plan within the organization.

Several parallel activities are involved in the preparation of an audit plan: scheduling the audit, notifying the auditee, and lining up audit resources. Once the audit plan is prepared, it is formally communicated to the auditee. The lead auditor should publish the audit plan; notify the client and the auditee of the impending audit; and confirm that any special needs or plans, such as travel requirements and security clearances, have been arranged.

Once these steps have been completed, the performance stage of the audit is ready to begin.

Mr. Dale Smith   February 23, 199X
ABC Industries
1 ABC Blvd.
City, State, 9900X

Dear Dale:

The audit team will perform a quality system audit of the ABC facility
to assess conformance to ANSI/ISO/ASQC Q9002:1994 standard
requirements. The scope of the audit will be limited to the requirements
stated in ISO 9002 (ANSI/ISO/ASQC Q9002) and existing internal
quality system standards. The audit process will be conducted according to recognized auditing conventions (as defined for ASQC Certified
Quality Auditors).

You should plan for the audit to require two days of on-site interviewing and verifying of requirements. A draft report will be left after the
audit, and the final report will be forwarded within two business days.
The auditors will be Jane Doe and myself.

The on-site audit is scheduled for March 23rd through March 24th.
The audit team will need a room with a table, telephone, and electrical
outlets (for computers and printers). The audit plan is enclosed.

As agreed, please forward the quality manual to my attention to arrive
no later than two weeks before the scheduled audit.

Thank you for your cooperation in making the necessary arrangements
to the planned quality audit.

                                            Sincerely,

                                            John Doe
                                            ASQC CQA

                                            Chip Jones
                                            Client

Copy: Chip Jones
        Jane Doe
Enclosures: 1

Figure 11.2. Notification letter.

SIDEBAR

Problems Commonly Encountered
During the Audit Planning Stage

Problems likely to be encountered during the planning stage of an audit include difficulties related to the availability of personnel and other audit resources and scheduling the audit.

Availability of Personnel. A common detriment or hindrance to effective planning for an internal audit is the reluctance of some organizations to release their people to do effective audit planning. Most audit team members are not full-time members of a quality assurance staff or of an auditing organization. They are either volunteers or people drafted from other areas of the company, such as production, accounting, sales, and personnel. It is often difficult for them to find the time that is needed to effectively plan an audit—generally four to six hours of the individual's time.

Availability of Other Resources. In addition to personnel problems, the availability of other resources, such as funding, can have an effect on audit planning. Also, the auditee may fail to forward the necessary documents (such as the quality manual) to the auditor in time to allow for adequate preparation.

Scheduling Difficulties. Often other events take priority and make the audit difficult to schedule. Such events could include a major reorganization or merger. Perhaps the auditee has just received a major contract, or the audit is scheduled at the same time that a regulatory agency plans a visit. The audit is an important event, but sometimes other events take higher priority.

Part III

Audit Performance

Chapter 12
Conducting the Opening Meeting

The performance phase of an audit is the actual fieldwork. It is the data-gathering portion of the audit that covers the time from the auditor's arrival at the audit location through the exit meeting.[1]

Soon after the arrival of the audit team at the audit site, the audit team and auditee gather for an opening meeting, sometimes called a pre-audit conference or entrance meeting. This meeting starts the data-gathering phase of the audit.

The principal objectives of the opening meeting are to accomplish the following:

- Introduce audit team members to auditee management

- Circulate an attendance roster

- Establish communication links

- Clarify the audit plan by reviewing/restating the scope and objective of the audit, as well as the reference standards being audited against; summarizing methods and procedures to be used during the audit

- Confirm logistics: hours, escorts, tentative schedules, needed facilities (for example, meeting rooms) and resources are available for audit team use

- Confirm time and date for closing meeting, as well as any interim meetings

Additionally, if applicable, the opening meeting may

- Include a review of previous audits' observations and corrective actions.

- Help ensure that the audit team understands the confidentiality agreement.

The opening meeting establishes the best climate for developing rapport and sets the ground rules for conducting an audit. Before an audit starts, individuals should know the daily audit schedule and know what to expect in the closing meeting, written report, corrective action requests, and any possible follow-up. The formality of the opening meeting should be flexible and may depend on many factors, including the audit scope, the size of the audit team, and whether the audit is internal or external.[2]

While an opening meeting should always take place, for the internal audit it is often a very short and informal meeting. Often there is more interaction between the audit team and management in the preparation stage for internal audits. Internal audits usually occur on a fairly regular basis, and all of the parties involved understand well what will be examined before the audit takes place.

ROLES AND RESPONSIBILITIES OF AN AUDITOR

The entire audit team should attend the opening meeting, which is conducted by the lead auditor. The lead auditor prepares the meeting agenda and often hands out agenda copies in advance.

At the opening meeting, the lead auditor

- Introduces audit team members and presents their credentials

- Restates the purpose and scope of the audit in a clear and diplomatic fashion; may refer to previous audits of a facility and any previously required corrective action

- Reinforces study during preparation phase by asking specific questions

- Solicits areas of interest from auditee or mentions areas of specific concern

- May present the audit checklist to the auditee (if not done earlier)
- Sets the detailed audit schedule (see Figure 12.1 for an example)
- Describes the quality-related documentation used to develop the audit plan

The lead auditor should also describe the audit process and the anticipated benefits. The lead auditor should allow time in the schedule to answer any questions from auditee personnel.

ROLES AND RESPONSIBILITIES OF AN AUDITEE

The appropriate members of an auditee's staff should attend the opening meeting, with at least one representative of management attending. Other responsible and interested parties, such as the supervisors or managers of the areas to be audited, may attend. The lead auditor may request minimum attendance, but should not limit it.[3] The ISO 10011 standard indicates that the auditee's senior management should attend the opening meeting.

A representative for the auditee introduces the people in attendance and "achieves consensus on the following points:

- The individual to represent the auditee on all matters during the audit
- Auditor access to areas and activities to be audited

Item/ element	Area/ function	Contact	Auditor	Time
Opening meeting	Conference room	All	All	9:00–9:30 A.M.
Document control	Quality assurance	Ms. Apostrophe	Mr. Brackets	10:00–11:00 A.M.
Order review	Marketing	Mr. Colon	Ms. Dash	10:00–11:00 A.M.
Design control	Research and development	Ms. Parentheses	Mr. Brackets	11:00 A.M.– 12:00 P.M.

Figure 12.1. Detailed audit schedule.

- Facilities to be provided for the audit team's use
- Support personnel to be provided: escorts, specialists, line personnel, etc.
- Safety and regulatory requirements
- Protection of proprietary rights"[4]

If members of an auditee's staff disagree with or need clarification on any of the lead auditor's statements, they should express an opinion or ask for clarification at this time. For example, if an auditor's stated scope for an audit does not match the auditee's expectations, the auditee must point out this fact at the opening meeting, rather than during or on completion of the audit.

Sometimes an auditee may wish to give a presentation to acquaint the auditor with the firm or a plant tour to familiarize the auditor with the facility. Brief presentations or tours are permissible, and at times highly desirable; but if the time spent on these activities becomes excessive, it is the lead auditor's responsibility to politely halt the proceedings so that the audit schedule remains intact. The following examples suggest different statements an auditor may make when an audit is not moving along as planned.

> I'm really enjoying this conversation, but all of us have a lot to do; so what do you say we get started.

> This tour has been very helpful, but I think it has accomplished what I needed; so let's start the audit interviews.

> Since we have so many areas to cover today, can we speed things up so we don't have to stay after working hours to complete the audit?

> What is next on the schedule? [The auditee notes the next step from the provided copy of the audit agenda.] Okay, let's move on so that we do not slow down the manufacturing process.

Finally, an auditee should provide an escort for each subgroup of the audit team. (An exception can be made for internal audits, if the auditor is already familiar with the organization and activities being audited.) The escort accompanies the auditor on the entire data-gathering portion of the audit and serves as a liaison between the auditing organization and auditee management. The escort fulfills the following roles.

- Performs personnel introductions and provides clarifying information as needed. For example, an escort can suggest a way of rephrasing a question, perhaps by substituting terminology more familiar ("local language") to the person being interviewed.

- Provides or requests supplies, records, etc., required by the auditor.

- Acts as an observer for management and, during daily briefings with management, provides an overview of the auditor's observations, findings, and conclusions.

- Acts as a guide for the auditor and may confirm or deny that a discrepancy or nonconformity has been found before moving on to the next area to be audited.

- Ensures that auditors comply with company rules, including safety rules.

Chapter 13
Audit Team Management

An audit team should employ one, or a combination of several, auditing strategies during the data-gathering phase of an audit. As data are gathered, the audit team should reassemble periodically to sort the data and to form tentative conclusions. If the data that have been gathered are unclear or contradictory, the audit team should determine the need for additional data that can be used to confirm or deny tentative conclusions. The audit team is also responsible for ensuring that an auditee representative (and/or escort) is made aware of potential problems as they surface.

GENERAL AUDITING STRATEGIES

Regardless of whether a product, process, or system is being audited, the auditor should use a general auditing strategy, or audit path, so that data are collected in a logical and methodical manner. Effective audit planning ensures that an auditor will have the time and means to conduct a thorough investigation of the audited organization. It also enables the auditor to segment the audit by element or department, or to use the discovery method or tracing techniques to gather data. Adhering to such strategies helps an auditor gain insight into the practices actually employed throughout a company and assists in the identification of problems.

Some functions/departments lend themselves naturally to one particular auditing strategy. For example, tracing techniques may be suitable in situations where there is a natural flow of work, such as in production areas.[1]

Tracing

Tracing, or following the chronological progress of something as it is processed, is a common and effective means of collecting objective evidence during an audit. In *forward* tracing, an auditor starts at the beginning or middle of a manufacturing process, for example, and traces forward. In *backwards tracing,* the auditor starts at the middle or end of a process and traces backward. Backwards tracing can be more revealing than forward tracing, because the auditor examines the process from a different perspective. A flowchart can be used as a road map for tracing activities. The auditor should

- Start at the beginning, middle, or end of the process.

- Choose an action, such as painting a wall, stamping, or folding.

- Gather information in six areas—labor, equipment, method, material, environment, and measurement—for the action chosen and record this information on a checklist. (These factors are discussed in Chapter 21.)

- Follow the path of the transaction backward or forward through the process.[2]

Discovery Method

The discovery method is sometimes called *random auditing*. This method investigates what is currently taking place and, therefore, reflects prevailing work procedures. However, the discovery method offers no discernible pattern to an audit, and an auditor can become disoriented or spend too much time in the facility.[3]

In most situations, the discovery method should not have to be used if the audit has been planned adequately. However, this method could be effective if the auditor knows that a problem exists but has not yet located it. By going in and looking around, an auditor may be able to bring the problem to the surface.

Element Method

The element method is a commonly employed auditing strategy. While it is usually interpreted as referring to ISO 9001 and the 20 elements of the standard, in reality the element method can refer to any element of any quality assurance standard or of the auditee's quality program. The auditor examines each element individually to see how it affects the entire system. This method is very thorough and good to use on an annual basis. However, when an audit team is very large or is spending several weeks in a facility, the element method can become very cumbersome.

Department Method

The department method is another way of dividing an auditing task and works especially well when the entity being audited is small. The auditor focuses on the entire operations of one department, rather than on segments of it, by reviewing numerous quality elements within that department. This auditing strategy touches on almost everything in an audited facility. While this is an excellent strategy when the audit team wishes to "slice the apple a different way," it should not be overused. Focusing too much on just one small group of people may not accurately represent what is happening throughout an organization.

MANAGEMENT OF THE AUDIT TEAM

As the audit progresses, separate daily meetings, sometimes called daily briefings, are held to update the audit team and auditee as to what information has been collected so far. These meetings are used to identify significant problems needing immediate attention and to clarify the information gathered.[4]

Communication Between Audit Team Members

The audit team should reconvene in a quiet portion of the facility or in a conference room at least once daily throughout an audit. Some teams prefer to hold daily meetings in the morning, while others prefer to hold them before lunch or at the end of the day. The timing of the meeting is less important than the topics discussed.

First, audit team members share the information gathered so far. Then, team members propose conclusions or identify potential problem areas on the basis of the information gathered. If contradictory information has been gathered or if team members disagree about what has been observed, then the team must gather additional information. Finally, in an effort to keep the audit on schedule, the audit team discusses what areas may need more or less attention than originally thought. This discussion redirects or modifies the remaining audit schedule, which helps keep the audit on track and prevents the audit team from becoming distracted by minor issues.

Between meetings, the audit team members are "on their own." If a team member runs into a problem during the audit or is uncertain as to how to handle a situation, the lead auditor should be contacted immediately.

In summary, daily meetings help an audit team to (1) identify possible areas for findings and determine how they might relate to other areas, (2) plan for the next day, and (3) prepare for its daily meeting with the auditee.

Communication with the Auditee

At the beginning or end of each day, the audit team should meet with the auditee to discuss what has been completed and what it planned. This meeting gives the lead auditor an opportunity to explain what has been looked at, what will be observed next, and where problems may exist.

Communicating potential findings every day serves two purposes. First, the auditee can communicate potential findings up the command chain so that auditee management is aware of problems before the closing meeting. Second, the auditee can either confirm or deny that a problem exists. An auditee who insists that a problem does not exist can offer more data in an attempt to convince the auditor that there is not a problem.

A formal daily meeting of the audit team and auditee is always recommended to help prevent difficult situations, such as auditee management refusing to accept the audit team's findings at the closing meeting. If an auditee will not agree to a daily meeting, the lead auditor must take responsibility for informing the escort and area supervisors of potential findings in an area.

Chapter 14
Audit Implementation

The data-gathering process normally takes most of the time and effort in the performance phase of an audit. The job of an auditor is to collect factual information, analyze and evaluate it in terms of the specified requirements, draw conclusions from this comparison, and report the results to management.[1]

METHODS OF DATA COLLECTION

In auditing, information, or objective evidence, can be gathered in one of several ways. The auditor may observe work in progress, interview employees or others involved in the activity being audited, or physically examine samples of product or supporting documentation.

Objective evidence can be qualitative or quantitative. These differences are discussed in Chapter 1.

The auditor must sort and summarize the objective evidence gathered (observations) into a format that will be useful to the client and/or auditee. The objective evidence is evaluated to determine if system controls are effective and efficient.

Techniques Used in Interviews

Interviewing—the process of obtaining information from another person in response to questions—is the most important and widely used form of data collection in auditing.

Interviews are normally conducted one-on-one; but an audit team may occasionally find it necessary to interview groups of individuals, or to conduct interviews by telephone or remote devices, such as videoconferencing. While one-on-one, face-to-face interviews are preferable for obtaining information, other methods may be appropriate in cost-versus-benefit situations.

Interviews are used in audits to gain insights, clarify information, confirm or deny suspicions, and elicit details that may not be brought out by other audit activities.[2] Dennis Arter has suggested a six-step interview process developed by Frank X. Brown.[3]

1. Put the interviewee at ease.

2. Explain your purpose.

3. Find out what they are doing.

4. Analyze what they are doing.

5. Make a tentative conclusion.

6. Explain your next step.

When conducting an interview, an auditor should begin by introducing himself or herself and putting the interviewee at ease. The purpose of the interview should be explained, followed by general, open-ended questions that get an interviewee talking about the job. An auditor may simply say, "What are you doing?" or "What tells you to do that?" If the interviewee's answers confirm the documentation, then the information has been corroborated. If not, then the auditor needs to probe by asking more specific questions to ascertain if a work problem does indeed exist, or whether the interview is hampered by miscommunication. An auditor may not understand the process the interviewee describes, or the interviewee may misinterpret or fail to understand a question. An escort can often help clarify communication problems resulting from unfamiliar terminology by rephrasing a question. However, an escort should not be permitted to answer for an interviewee.

As an auditor concludes whether necessary controls are in place, those preliminary conclusions should be communicated to the interviewee and/or escort. For example, an auditor could say, "That's good. It looks to me as though you have a thorough understanding of the requirements of your job and are doing good work." An auditor who suspects a potential finding could say, "It looks like we might have a problem in this area. I can't see where those controls are placed." Such comments give the interviewee an opportunity to offer more information. If the interviewee allays the auditor's concerns, no problem exists.

The auditor usually takes notes throughout an interview and should take a few minutes at the end of each interview to ensure that the notes will be complete and meaningful when reviewed later in the day. If extensive note-taking is necessary, it may be best for the auditor to step out of the room or into a secluded location to record observations since the interviewee may become unnerved by the auditor recording large amounts of information.

In all communications with the auditee, the auditor must focus on the situation, issues, documentation, activities, and/or behavior—not on the person. When communicating with auditee management, the auditor should avoid naming individuals whenever possible.

People respond readily to inquiries and offer helpful suggestions for improvements if they feel the audit team is sincere, appreciates their views, and has their needs and interests at heart. Each person involved with an organization has a unique perspective, as does each member of the audit team. One person can filter information differently from another, miss an angle, or stop short of getting the full story.[4] For these reasons, facts stated and other data collected during an audit interview must be corroborated to ensure accuracy. The information can be corroborated in one of three ways.

1. Another person, preferably from another group or management level, says the same thing.

2. Another member of the audit team hears the same thing (from the same or different source).

3. An item, document, or record verifies the action.[5]

An auditor should be aware that certain types of problems may occur during interviews and should be trained in techniques that minimize such interferences.

• *The auditee may attempt to steer the auditor toward specific interviewees.* Often an auditee would prefer that the auditor interview certain personnel during an audit and avoid certain others. However, this person's knowledge may not be typical of others in the organization. Therefore, the auditor should take charge of the selection process.

An auditor should approach an area and look around to see who is doing what jobs. Candidates for interviews can be randomly chosen as long as it is safe to interrupt them in their jobs.

If an auditee insists that a specific person is unavailable for interviewing, the auditor should be considerate but persistent if the interview is vital to the success of the audit. Without being threatening, the auditor can suggest that the person's unavailability may prolong the audit. A statement such as "I may have to stay over for another shift" may gain an auditor the desired cooperation.

• *The escort or area supervisor may answer for the interviewee or intimidate him or her.* Problems may result if an audit escort or area supervisor attempts to answer for an interviewee. In addition, an escort's presence may threaten or intimidate the interviewee. An escort generally stays within listening distance and takes notes, but should step back slightly. An ideal arrangement is for an auditor to sit (or stand) between the interviewee and escort, facing the interviewee.

An escort is to be an observer only and should not be involved in the interview unless there are communication problems. An auditor can minimize an escort's participation in the interview by directing questions to, and maintaining eye contact with, the interviewee. Another technique is to ask task-specific questions such as questions about machine setups and the measuring of parameters that are normally beyond the knowledge of an escort.

If an escort starts to answer for an auditee, the auditor needs to redirect the question to the interviewee, avoiding eye contact with the escort. If an escort continues to interfere, an auditor should say, "I prefer to get the information from the staff member."

• *The auditor may ask leading questions, expecting to hear certain answers.* An auditor should not lead an interviewee with the questioning. Leading questions can be avoided if the auditor asks open-ended

The auditor should say . . .	Not . . .
How (where, when, who, what, why) do you record the test results?	Do you record the test results in the lab log book?
How do you know this value is right?	This instrument is calibrated, isn't it?
What is the first thing you do?	First you set up the equipment, right?
How do you know this is the current (correct) version of the drawing?	Is this drawing current (correct)?
How were you trained to perform this procedure?	Did you read the standard operating procedure during training?
What are the reporting requirements for nonconformances?	Don't you have to notify your supervisor whenever a nonconformance occurs?
What is the standard procedure for responding to customer complaints?	When a customer calls, don't you have to record the details on form X?
Is this equipment calibrated? How do you know?	Does this sticker indicate that the equipment is calibrated?
How do you know how to do this operation?	Do you follow the procedure for this operation?
What do you do with the finished product?	Do you place the finished product on the rack?

Figure 14.1. Open-ended questions contrasted with closed-ended questions.

questions such as those described in Figure 14.1. Additionally, if an auditor goes into an interview expecting to hear certain answers, the audit results likely will be biased.

• *Communication problems or other conflicts may occur between the auditor and interviewee.* Communication problems are probably the principal difficulty that must be overcome during an audit. An auditor can minimize the effects of miscommunication by relying on the escort to correct any misunderstandings and by corroborating all information through one of the methods already mentioned.

An auditor who does not have a good grasp of the process being audited may not ask the right questions and may realize only after completing the interview that important issues were not addressed. Daily meetings help bring this type of situation to an auditor's attention.

Other types of conflicts may include employees who are hostile to anyone in authority. Also, sometimes interviewees may be unable to concentrate because they are distracted by the fact that their jobs are not getting done. People are afraid to say, "I am very busy. I need to complete this test. Can you come back in 10 minutes?" A good auditor will sense when an interviewee is preoccupied, move off, then find other ways to keep the audit moving. Additionally, the auditor should guard against reacting improperly to employees who have "hidden agendas" or "axes to grind."

How Are Collected Data Used?
Auditors gather data as objective evidence to determine the degree of conformance to quality objectives and/or standards and to identify areas for continuous improvement. The main uses of gathered data are for analysis, detection, summary, verification, and presentation.

Analysis. Analysis is the evaluation of information and data gathered during the audit for the purpose of determining compliance to a requirement. This evaluation may be the result of the auditor's professional judgment, or the auditor may use statistical techniques. The auditor needs to be able to apply good judgment as well as have a working knowledge of statistical analysis techniques. Whatever the method of evaluation or analysis used, the auditor must ensure that decisions made from data and information gathered during the course of the audit stand up to scrutiny by others.

Detection. Some observations constitute a "finding" in the eyes of an auditor. The evaluation method used by the auditor must be able to detect abnormalities in the data and in the source(s) of the data. What is the limit or minimum that you as an auditor can or will accept? For example, how many defects must be found before something becomes a reportable observation? The determination of "minor" and "major" from the auditor's point of view may be based on input from the audit manager and others.

Summary. An auditor must be able to summarize the results of data analysis into a unified statement about the adequacy and effectiveness of the process represented by the analyzed data. The auditor should examine patterns or trends and consolidate similar observations into a single finding.

Verification. Prior to presentation to the auditee as final results, the analysis or judgment and summary should be reviewed by all members of the audit team to verify the accuracy of the analyzed data and the decisions made from the data. In the event of a conflict between members of the audit team as to the acceptability of the audit results, the lead auditor is responsible for resolving all issues and determining what should be reported. The other members of the audit team must support the decision of the lead auditor. Verification is done primarily to prevent errors in the reporting of audit results.

Presentation. The facts of an audit are presented at the closing meeting and in the final audit report. The method of presentation depends on the type of data analysis used. If an auditor judges the data collected, rather than analyzing it, the results should not be presented as statistical "facts." The reporting method should enable the auditee to take proper corrective action and not pursue nonexistent or unimportant issues.

VERIFICATION OF DOCUMENTATION

An auditor must be well-trained in methods for verifying documentation. Documentation includes *documents,* which are written instructions that establish a practice or direct a person how to do a job. In contrast, *records* result from a particular step or process being performed as directed in the documents. A document specifies what *should* be done; a record specifies what *has* been done.

Documents direct people how to do things. Examples of documents include written work instructions, purchase orders to a supplier, procedures, diagrams, drawings, and blank forms. (Refer to Chapter 8 for a list of additional documents.) Records are evidence that practices outlined in documents have been performed. Thus, records verify that the actions specified in documents have indeed taken place as required.

Reasons for Verifying Documents and Records

Documents and records must be verified for the following reasons.

- To ensure accuracy. Information may be (unintentionally) incomplete or incorrect.

- To illustrate that the person filling out the record has an understanding of what is to be recorded.

- To eliminate fraud (intentional). An auditor must attempt to verify that audit documents and records are truthful and that there has been no intent to deceive others or misrepresent facts.

Methods for Verifying Documents and Records

To ensure that documents and records reflect actual practice, an auditor should verify that they are secure, permanent, current, and accurate. As defined in this handbook, a document tells someone what to do and a record is evidence that they did it.

Records should be protected so that they are not accessible to unauthorized personnel. Databases need to be controlled so that only authorized persons can modify important records. Records should be backed up or stored in more than one location. Documentation should be permanent—written in ink, unless environmental circumstances do not allow for the recording of data with ink. For example, some chemicals used in laboratories may cause reactions when they come in contact with ink, so an alternate means of recording data would be permissible in this or other special circumstances. If records must be changed, the changes should be dated and signed or initialed. The original information should be kept intact so that the new information and the reason for the change can be assessed. Erasures or "white out" fluid are strictly forbidden on records.

Documents should be current and available to the people who need them. Sometimes what an auditor sees on the production floor does not match expectations based on the documentation because it has not been updated as procedures have changed.

Some documents and records reside in computer programs. Access to and changes to documents, as well as the computer code changes, must be controlled. For records, controls should be in place to limit who can access records, enter data as a record, control record changes, and control code changes to the software.

Documents and records are verified primarily through three means: tracing, sampling, and physical examination.

Tracing. Documents are traced as a means of verification. An auditor reads the audit procedure and observes others attempting to accomplish the procedure. If it cannot be done, the auditor needs to determine whether the procedure is inaccurate (which could indicate that the person who wrote the procedure did not understand the process or that the process has been changed and the document has not been updated) or whether the process is being improperly performed (which could indicate that employees have not been adequately trained).

Sampling. Documents and records can be sampled to verify that they are accurate. For example, an auditor reads a document that says "do this" and goes out into a couple of places where "this" is being done and asks, "Did you do this?" In the case of records, an auditor can sample portions of a record by verifying that the recorded result occurred. This verification can be done by talking to the person who recorded the information or by alternate means, such as by requesting records from the escort or management representative.

Physical Examination. Physical examination refers to one-to-one examinations of items to verify information. For example, if a record says "This cabinet was painted blue," then the auditor may examine the item to see if it is indeed blue.

PRINCIPLES AND PRACTICES OF CALIBRATION

Data must be precise and accurate so that an auditor can form reliable conclusions. An auditee's instruments must be capable of providing data of the precision and accuracy needed for the types of decisions to be made. Machines and equipment must be calibrated and maintained so that they continue to provide usable data. An auditor needs to verify that data-generating equipment has been calibrated.

Calibration is the process of comparing an instrument to standards and determining the accuracy of the instrument. Auditors verify calibration stickers and applicable documentation. Calibration is normally scheduled on a database, and an auditor looks for discrepancies between the calibration schedule and the applicable calibration records.

In addition to defining accuracy and precision limits, an auditee's calibration procedures must address the issue of remedial action if equipment is found to be out of calibration. In other words, how did the out-of-calibration equipment affect the products that were manufactured or tested with that piece of equipment? If necessary, production may be halted or a product recall may be issued.

Calibration systems are normally patterned after national or international calibration standards. In the United States, five ANSI/ASQC or ISO standards or draft standards are supported by the ASQC Measurement Quality Division.

- ANSI/ASQC M1-1996, *American National Standard for Calibration Systems*

- ANSI/ASQC M2-199X Draft, *American National Standard for Quality Control of Measurements*

- ISO 10012-1:1992, *Metrological Confirmation System for Measuring Equipment*

- ISO/DIS 10012-2, *Control of Measurement Processes*

- ANSI/NCSL Z540-1-1994, *American National Standard for Calibration—Calibration Laboratories and Measuring and Test Equipment—General Requirements*[6]

An audited company should have an effective metrology and calibration system for standards, measuring, and test equipment. The company should provide and maintain measuring and testing devices to ensure that hardware, software, and services conform to technical requirements. In some cases, companies require employees and inspectors to provide their own tools or test equipment and to submit them to the company's calibration procedures. The objective of the system is to ensure that inspection and test equipment is adjusted, replaced, or repaired before it becomes inaccurate. The system should consist of the following elements.

- Labels, tags, color codes, or other means of tracing the measurement device to the individual calibration record.

- A requirement for calibration practices.

- Certified primary company or reference standards traceable to industry, national, or international standards such as those of the National Institute of Standards and Technology.

- Listings by department of calibration status and delinquents. Instruments that are out of calibration cannot be used to certify product and must be removed from service until calibrated.

- All personally owned tools used should be in the system and calibrated.

- Inspection department should have calibration as an inspection check before "buying" off on items[7] (that is, before accepting or believing them).

Standardization is the ability of a piece of equipment to produce similar results each time it is used and may include external adjustments of the equipment to conform to known standards. Calibration is a formal system of standardization and may require internal adjustments of the machine to conform to industrial or recognized national standards, such as those provided by the National Institute of Standards and Technology.[8]

In a good calibration/standardization program, written procedures and work instructions cover such items as how to calibrate, frequency of calibration, and how to measure.[9] Documented evidence of calibrations may be required by the documentation and/or standard being used. In some service industries, calibration does not exist.

Chapter 15
Audit Analysis

Throughout the course of an audit, team members continually attempt to analyze data as they are gathered. In their daily meetings, team members attempt to examine, sort, and verify evidence. If information appears to be contradictory, the audit team seeks more data to confirm or deny a position.

Once the data-gathering phase is closed, audit team members meet a final time to analyze and classify the evidence collected before presenting audit results to the auditee at the closing meeting.

Before the closing meeting, the audit team sorts and discusses all facts uncovered during the audit. Each finding must be a clear, concise statement of a general problem (for example, "Work instruction documents are not effectively controlled. This could cause cost overruns and schedule delays"). Each finding statement should be followed by a brief restatement of the particular control element that is in need of attention (in this example the quality program requirement for controlling documents). Then the individual facts that show the basis for the statement should be listed and numbered.[1]

At its final gathering before the closing meeting, the audit team members do a subjective evaluation of the accumulated data: Sort the data, see what supports them and what they support, and look at the data again away from the situation to see what they mean. Any finding should be clear to a reasonable person. The auditor has to look at the evidence found, its relation to the purpose of the audit, and its importance to the entire scheme that has been audited.

If it appears that contradictory evidence has been gathered and the audit team cannot gather additional data, the contradiction should be included in the audit report as a finding or observation, and clarification should be requested. A supplemental report can be generated if necessary to clarify the original audit report.

Through analysis of audit data, the audit team distinguishes between chronic and isolated incidents, classifies nonconformances and noncompliances, and determines the effectiveness of controls.

DISTINGUISHING BETWEEN CHRONIC AND ISOLATED INCIDENTS

When accumulating data, an auditor can examine trends and patterns to determine whether an incident is chronic or isolated.

An auditor who detects a possible problem looks for a recurrence (that is, gathers additional data). If subsequent data shows recurrence of the incident in several places, it is a chronic incident.

For example, if one piece of equipment is overdue for calibration by about a month, but all other equipment is in calibration, the auditee may have a good calibration program and the one piece of equipment is an isolated case. However, if a high percentage of equipment has not been calibrated on schedule, the problem is chronic (major).

Thus, an auditor needs to look at things from a system standpoint and try to assess how the overall system is working. If well-documented procedures exist, and an audit is confirming the procedure, while only one or two problems exist that do not affect the integrity of the product, then the problem is isolated. Just one occurrence of a major problem, on the other hand, may be significant enough to make it a systemic problem.

If after a preliminary evaluation of data a problem appears to be chronic, the auditor should go back and draw another sample. Once it has been determined whether a problem is a chronic or isolated event, it can be classified for reporting purposes as either a finding (major) or an observation (minor).

CLASSIFYING NONCONFORMANCES AND NONCOMPLIANCES

An auditor must sort and classify facts based on the severity of the problem, frequency of occurrence, and the risks associated with it. The most critical (major) problems are often called *findings*. This term can apply to noncompliances or nonconformances. A *noncompliance* is process associated and specifies that the action or activity did not meet certain requirements. A *nonconformity* is product related and indicates that the product or certain characteristics of the product do not meet requirements. In common practice the terms *noncompliance* and *nonconformity* are used interchangeably. Chronic problems are usually reported as findings. However, even an isolated incident can be considered a finding if its impact on the overall quality system is great.

Minor problems are often called observations or concerns. Such problems usually do not denote a system breakdown, but could result in one in the future if not properly corrected or contained.

The method used to classify audit results varies from organization to organization. Some organizations classify findings as major or as category 1 findings, while observations are classified as minor or category 2 findings. ISO 10011 states that the auditor will report audit results as observations and identify which observations are to be considered "nonconformities." Some auditors further subdivide nonconformities as major or minor.

The most serious problems need the auditee's urgent attention, while the less important ones are treated with a time frame and priority that they deserve. If the auditee needs additional time to analyze the root cause of a serious problem, the auditor should allow it. The timing of corrective action is dependent on its importance, complexity, and the availability of the resources needed to take corrective action.

MEASURING THE EFFECTIVENESS OF CONTROLS

Some audits measure not only compliance, but also the adequacy and effectiveness of the controls that are in place. If a control is attempting to achieve a certain result, how does an auditor measure if the desired outcome is being achieved? The presence of damaged material in a warehouse indicates that material handling procedures may be ineffective, the use of nonconforming material in finished product indicates poor control of nonconforming material, obsolete drawings and procedures in a manufacturing area indicate that the document control system is ineffective, etc.

An auditor can get an indication of the effectiveness of controls by the nature and number of nonconformances observed.

The final team meeting is held after improvement areas have been identified and just prior to the closing meeting. The team collects all information and identifies significant areas to be mentioned at the closing meeting. The team

- Decides on the contents and emphasis of the report

- Outlines major findings and discoveries

- Finalizes list of improvement areas

- Lists any outstanding items or questions[2]

Based on the conclusions formed at this meeting, the lead auditor prepares a preliminary draft of the audit report. The draft report can be handwritten or typed on a computer and then photocopied or printed.

Chapter 16
Closing Meeting

The closing meeting, sometimes called a post-audit conference or exit meeting, ends the performance stage of an audit. At the closing meeting the lead auditor presents a draft or preliminary audit report to the auditee.

The closing meeting is a presentation of the audit results to the auditee organization and, in some cases, the client. The client may choose not to attend the closing meeting so that the auditor is giving the auditee a preliminary view of the information to be provided to the client. The purpose of the closing meeting is to present audit observations to senior management to ensure that audit results are clearly understood. The closing meeting normally takes place following the conclusion of the interviews and the final team meeting.

The lead auditor may circulate an attendance roster for the closing meeting, which includes the audit team, at least one management representative from the auditee, and other personnel deemed appropriate by auditee management. For example, the escort may be present to help explain details of findings. Usually the same people attend that attended the opening meeting. Sometimes higher levels of management attend since they want to be informed of the audit results. The lead auditor should do most of the talking, and a member of the audit team should keep minutes of the meeting. The minutes should include any agreed-upon changes to the audit report.

Individual auditors may present their own findings, or the lead auditor may present all findings and rely on the appropriate auditor to clarify and answer questions. Any discussions should be kept brief and pertinent and should clarify the audit findings, not justify the audit method.[1] Finally, the lead auditor should present the audit team's conclusions about the quality system's overall effectiveness.

ROLES AND RESPONSIBILITIES OF AN AUDITOR

The closing meeting is conducted by the lead auditor, who should

- Present the summary.
- Read the results of the audit without interruption from the auditee.
- Discuss audit details; individual auditors may clarify statements or respond to specific questions of the areas they have audited.
- Indicate how audit results are categorized and prioritized.
- Explain the required follow-up and expected corrective action response.[2]
- Ensure that minutes and an attendance record are kept.

A big problem at closing meetings occurs when communication between an auditor and auditee did not get reported to the top of the command chain beforehand. The auditee, caught off guard, may become defensive. Daily meetings help prevent this problem. If an auditee does not want daily meetings, the auditor can prevent problems by promoting communication during the audit. An auditor who suspects that information is not getting to the top should casually, but deliberately, inform management of audit results as issues are uncovered.

The formal, official audit report should be issued to the auditee by the client or lead auditor within the time period previously agreed to or specified by organization procedure. Many organizations specify that audit reports be received within two weeks. More than 30 days between conclusion of the performance stage and issuance of the audit report is usually considered excessive.

ROLES AND RESPONSIBILITIES OF AN AUDITEE

The closing meeting should be attended by senior managers of the areas that were audited. Attendance by several layers of management should be discouraged. It may lead to arguing and unproductive time, since employees often feel obligated to defend their positions to their supervisors.[3]

At the closing meeting, auditee representatives have the responsibility to listen attentively. There should be no extensive discussions unless the auditee needs clarification of items in the audit report.

If the auditee and auditor disagree as to whether a finding exists, or have different opinions on the degree of criticality of a finding, the auditee can present its view of the situation as part of its response to the requests for corrective action.

SIDEBAR

Problems Commonly Encountered
During the Audit Performance Stage

The following are examples of the types of problems commonly encountered during the performance stage of an audit.

Losing Track of Time or Scope. Problems regarding a lack of time or loss of focus or scope are frequently encountered during audits. Daily meetings that assess the audit's progress should help prevent such problems. Also, properly prepared working papers can help eliminate problems related to time management or the focus of the audit.

Unreasonable Absence or Unavailability of Key Personnel. An auditor needs to be able to work around the absence of key personnel. However, if this situation is happening regularly during an external audit, the auditor may need to call a meeting with management or stop the audit. If an obstruction exists and no mutual agreement can be reached at the meeting, then the auditor should report to the client for advice on how or whether to continue the audit. In an internal audit, people often take the availability of the audit team for granted. They may feel free to handle their own crises as they arise because they believe it should be easy for the audit team to reschedule.

Interference from Internal Problems. Employees sometimes wish to involve the audit team in internal problems. For example, if employees believe that their performance would improve with the addition of a certain piece of equipment, they may attempt to enlist the auditor in lobbying management for the purchase of such equipment.

Extensive Discussions or Arguments. The auditee may attempt to prolong the closing meeting with extensive discussion or arguments. The closing meeting is not a time for negotiation. The lead auditor should present the information contained in the draft audit report, make sure that the auditee understands the results and what is expected in the way of a corrective action plan, and then end the meeting.

Lack of Effective Communication. Communication barriers pose a great threat to the successful completion of an audit. This is why training in interviewing techniques is so important. Unless auditors can word questions in an unbiased and concise manner, they may not receive accurate responses. Corroborating information gathered through an interview is one method auditors use to help ensure that misunderstandings have not occurred.

Part IV

Audit Reporting, Corrective Action, Follow-Up, and Closure

Chapter 17
Reporting

After audit results have been reported orally and visually to the auditee at the closing meeting, the lead auditor formally communicates the audit results in a written audit report. While the audit team may have prepared a handwritten or typed report to present to the auditee at the closing meeting, this report should be clearly marked *draft* or *preliminary*. The closing meeting should have included discussion of all significant findings so that the auditee is not surprised by information in the final audit report. The final audit report, which is the document that formally communicates the audit results to the client and the auditee, is prepared, signed, and dated by the lead auditor. It should be reviewed and approved by the management of the auditing organization as well as the client before it is sent to the auditee.

The audit report should be sent to the auditee as soon as possible upon completion of the audit. As a general rule, no more than 30 days should elapse between the closing meeting and the auditee's receipt of the audit report, with less than two weeks being highly desirable. When a significant amount of time passes between the end of an audit and the issuance of the audit report, the urgency of the corrective action is diminished, misunderstandings or miscommunications are more likely to occur, the auditee may be less motivated to resolve problems, and the audit program may be viewed as inefficient.

An audit report serves the following functions.

- It supplies the user with needed, timely information for corrective action and control system improvement. The auditee must take corrective action or present an explanation for not doing so.

- It guides management and its consultants in subsequent decisions and activities.

- The written format ensures that results can be widely communicated, misunderstandings are reduced, public inspection is possible, and follow-up work is facilitated.[1]

CONTENTS OF AN AUDIT REPORT

While the format of the written audit report can vary widely from company to company or industry to industry, certain information always should be included. Most audit reports contain the following (or equivalent) sections: introduction, summary, listing of the significant observations (findings) and conclusions, and requests for corrective action.

An audit report should not name individual employees of the auditee in connection with specific findings or observations; a report should refer to positions, titles, or systems when identifying deficiencies.

There is no standard length for audit reports. However, reports should be concise and should contain prescribed information. One common arrangement is a two-page audit report with any findings and positive practices added as attachments.

Introduction
Much of the introductory material included in an audit report can be completed from the audit plan before the audit is performed. The audit report introduction

- States the purpose and scope of the audit
- Identifies the auditee, client, and auditing organization
- Identifies the audit team members and presents their qualifications

- Specifies the audit dates
- Specifies the standards used for the audit
- May list auditee personnel involved in or contacted during the audit
- Lists report distribution

Additionally, the audit report introduction may mention the auditee's audit history and discuss what records or documents were examined as part of the audit.

Summary

The summary, or abstract, section of the audit report is a synopsis of the audit results. It should include the following information.

- Statements pertaining to the observations of nonconformities
- The audit team's judgment of the extent of the auditee's compliance with the applicable standard
- The system's ability to achieve defined quality objectives

Results of the Audit

The next section of a formal report should include the following information.

- Audit findings/nonconformities and number.
- Specific requirement.
- Details or specifications of the nonconformity or finding.
- The auditor may offer recommendations (if required to do so by the client) for correcting deficiencies or improving the quality program. *Note: When the client requests recommendations from the auditor, the recommendations should be placed in an appendix or separate report since they may be distracting if presented in the audit results section of the audit report. Even when recommendations are included, it is the auditee's responsibility to implement the necessary changes.*
- Names of people contacted during the audit.

- Provisions for auditee's response.

- Provisions for recording corrective action and follow-up activities.

This section of the audit report should explain how the results of the audit are classified. The results of the audit may be indicated as findings, nonconformities, deficiencies, adverse conclusions, or significant observations and conclusions. The most common terminology used to report the results of an audit are *nonconformity* and *finding*. The terminology used should be defined to ensure the auditee's understanding. Observations made during the audit that violate a requirement should be reported and their importance should be taken into account. Within each category, further classifications of critical, major, and minor may exist.

Each problem area (finding, nonconformity) should be listed in one or two sentences. The report should include facts or examples that support or explain each finding or positive practice. The results of the audit may be listed in order of importance, in sequence of the procedure or performance standard clauses followed, or in no particular order. Noteworthy accomplishments or positive practices—processes that work exceptionally well—may be included and can be listed at the front or back of the report, depending on the auditor's preference. The auditor requires corrective action on findings (nonconformities) to meet the requirements of the client.

Some auditors may report "concerns" if requested by the client. Concerns are not a violation of a requirement, but rather are based on the auditor's experience and could develop into a problem if not corrected. For instance, some organizations have multiple document control systems; while that is not a nonconformity, it is typically not good practice. Nonconformities require formal, extensive corrective action, but a concern is something an auditee should review, discuss, and act on to prevent a nonconformity.

Concerns may simply be ideas to improve the process and, as such, can be a valuable addition to an audit. Concerns should be identified clearly as not binding as far as corrective action is concerned and/or should be reported in an appendix. If left uncorrected, though, a concern may turn into a finding on the next audit if deterioration of the system becomes obvious or nonconformities appear. In the report, an auditor should note that the findings are symptoms, the cause of which remains to be identified. Furthermore, wherever a problem is identified, other similar systems or those systems in the same area should also be examined.

Corrective Action Requests

Management of an audited organization should be requested to review and investigate the audit findings to determine the appropriate corrective action needed and should be asked to respond to the report in writing. The response should clearly state the corrective action planned or taken to prevent recurrence, if the finding is significant, and the scheduled completion date for the corrective action. If corrective action is not appropriate, the response should specify the reason for no action.[2]

All requests for corrective action should ask the auditee to determine the following:

- The root cause of the problem
- Long-term corrective action planned for the cause
- Short-term (remedial) action planned for each of the findings listed
- Schedules and responsibilities for these actions[3]

To prevent a nonconformity or problem from recurring, an auditor *(Note: or client, depending on the audit's purpose and scope and the delegated responsibility of the auditing organization. In some cases, the auditor may not have any responsibility for the corrective action phases of the audit. Especially in many third-party audits, the auditor may collect and interpret information and provide this information to the client, who in turn manages the corrective action phase. Therefore, it may be appropriate to substitute "client" for "auditor" here and in Chapter 18.)* will ask the auditee to give attention to and take action on certain items. Adverse findings may be documented on a separate sheet called a corrective action request or discrepancy notice. A corrective action request, a statement of what the condition should be and what it is, includes several examples of what occurred. Serious problems are normally supported by many incidences, but an auditor can also document single instances of major problems such as the lack of or total breakdown of a system. An auditor issues reports or corrective action requests for areas in which the auditee needs to take action. The auditee needs to identify and correct the root cause of the problem. Then the auditee should fix the symptoms or results of the root cause.

Normally, an audit report identifies an area of nonconformance in the auditee's system and does not contain detailed technical information about a proprietary process or material. Any confidential information that may appear in an auditor's notes or in the completed checklist is retained by the auditor and must be protected to prevent disclosing a confidence. The official records contain a copy of a blank checklist, which does not contain proprietary information.

DISTRIBUTION OF AN AUDIT REPORT

The distribution list for an audit report should be noted on the report. The distribution of the audit report is at the discretion of the client unless this task has been delegated to the auditor or auditing organization. For an internal audit the report is normally distributed to the supervisor of the audited area as well as to someone in higher management. For an external audit, the report typically goes to a division manager or chief executive officer. In addition to the client and the auditee, the auditing organization maintains a copy of the report in its official files, and each member of the audit team also retains a copy.

An auditor should not send a report directly to the auditee unless requested to do so by the client. Rather, the report should be attached to a cover letter/memo issued by the client. This procedure promotes accountability of the auditing function.

When findings exist, the auditee should be asked to provide a corrective action plan stating how and when each problem will be fixed. An auditee must respond to an audit report in a reasonable time agreed on by the auditor and auditee. Many industry segments consider 30 days a reasonable time period. An auditee's response should include a corrective action plan for each finding, as well as a proposed time schedule for resolution of each item.

PRIORITIZING SIGNIFICANT OBSERVATIONS AND CONCLUSIONS

An auditor uses several techniques to prioritize observations before the closing meeting. Upon receipt of the formal audit report, an auditee may employ the same or similar techniques to determine which problems the organization should concentrate on correcting first, based on the significance or cost of the inefficiency. After making this determination, an auditee can focus on preparing a corrective action plan that addresses the remedial action or other action taken to eliminate the problem.

Pareto analysis, one method of prioritizing audit results, is discussed in detail in Part V of this handbook.

In any audit, risk is associated with reporting a finding on the basis of available data. An auditor may fail to identify a significant problem or may identify a problem that is not significant. Evaluation is often based on a relatively small sample, and therefore involves a large sampling risk.

The risk-benefit ratio is a method of analyzing the risk of reporting (based on the sample) or not reporting an area of concern compared to the benefit to be gained by reporting it. Criticality refers to the importance of an observation. If there is significant opportunity for project failure or a safety concern, a critical activity or item should be reported after one occurrence as opposed to multiple occurrences for an item of lesser importance.

The auditee's management is responsible for setting priorities on audit results. An auditee should draw conclusions in order to focus on those problems that provide the greatest benefit for the least effort and expense. As the group responsible for developing the corrective action plan, management needs to know what its resources are and what to fix first. In an internal audit, the auditor may be involved this step.

An auditee sets priorities by looking at the range of problems in relation to the entire system and noting where problems are clustering. Additionally, the auditee is responsible for recognizing the potential for similar conditions elsewhere in the organization or system and taking the necessary steps to rectify those problems. The quality system audit is not intended to identify each and every instance of a problem—it is not a 100 percent inspection activity. Rather, an audit looks for trends that might suggest a systemic problem.

Chapter 18
Corrective Action and Follow-Up

The auditee is responsible for implementing corrective action. Sometimes an auditee will look to the auditor for a solution or recommendation, but the auditor should proceed with caution when asked to do so. An auditor, while not precluded from providing a solution, may not have the technical knowledge to address and solve the problem. In addition, an auditor who gives a solution takes "ownership" of the problem. An auditor who has studied a process may have an excellent understanding of it and may be able to offer assistance to the auditee who seems genuinely confused about what is expected in the way of corrective action. It is important, however, that the auditee take responsibility for the solution. An auditor who participates in implementing or modifying a quality system compromises objectivity in regard to later audits of that area. For these reasons, many companies' auditors and most third-party auditors are often prohibited from recommending corrective action.

The auditee should prepare a corrective action plan and issue it to the auditor within a specified time, usually within 30 days of receiving the formal audit report. The first step in the development of a corrective action plan is the identification of the problem and the determination of the root cause. After a problem has been identified, the auditee may sometimes take immediate or short-term corrective action. Such action, usually considered remedial or temporary, is a quick containment action and is not necessarily the action needed to solve the problem permanently.

On the other hand, long-term corrective action is permanent and addresses the underlying cause. An auditee needs to implement a solution to ensure that the problem will not recur.

Once a deficiency and its root cause have been identified, the corrective action plan can be developed. The plan should cite action already taken to correct the deficiency and to preclude a similar occurrence on that and similar products. The plan should identify not only the action to be taken but also who is responsible for that action and by what date the preventive action will be in effect.[1]

When attempting to evaluate a proposed corrective action plan, an auditor should make sure the auditee is treating the problem, not a symptom of the problem. Will the proposed solution cause another problem? The proposed solution might address the issue on the surface but may not prevent the problems from recurring. Is the corrective action plan specific enough to ensure that changes will be permanent?

The principle of corrective action is that conditions adverse to quality must be identified and corrected. The cause must be determined. Steps must be taken to preclude repetition. True corrective action is difficult to implement, since the real causes of problems are seldom easy to identify.[2]

A five-step process is recommended for corrective action.

1. Document what the problem is and "stop the bleeding" (that is, implement immediate—remedial—corrective action).

2. Conduct an investigation to identify root causes.

3. Design, implement, and verify the effectiveness of the corrective action.

4. Ensure that the noncompliance is managed and controlled to avoid the potential of recurrence.

5. Analyze the effects of the findings on the product being manufactured, etc. For example, what, if anything, does the organization need to do (remedial actions) about products shipped or systems implemented while it was noncompliant?

Follow-up action may be accomplished through written communication, review of revised documents, re-audit after the reported implementation date, or other appropriate means.[3]

CRITERIA FOR ACCEPTABLE CORRECTIVE ACTION

Corrective action must be timely, effective, and prevent recurrence of the same problem (or the occurrence of a new one). A technical specialist may have to assess the proposed corrective action plan if the auditor does not have the expertise to do so.

If a problem is corrected, the auditor can close out that finding. If the audited organization does not want to take corrective action, it can maintain that the audit team has made an error and give additional information. Or the auditee can acknowledge that the corrective action request has been received, that it is understood, that more time is needed to work on it, and that a plan to address the problem will be prepared within two more weeks (or any specific time period).

The lead auditor coordinates the review of the corrective action request. The review may be conducted by the lead auditor or assigned to the individual auditor who found the problem. The lead auditor should agree with the recommendations for corrective action made by individual audit team members.

If the proposed corrective action plan seems feasible and reasonable, the auditor accepts it. Either the auditor or a designee can verify that the auditee is doing what has been promised and is meeting requirements of the corrective action. The auditor often follows up with a visit to the work area to check that corrective action has been implemented, to assess its effectiveness, and to confirm that it prevents recurrences of the problem.

Findings can be closed out individually. Some corrective actions take longer than others, and verification does not have to be done immediately. It can be combined with another trip if possible, or another auditor can be asked to verify and bring back the information. Corrective actions can be closed out as they are performed.

Corrective action must be timely. It is permissible for an auditee to request reasonable extensions, since auditors realize that some problems take more than 30 days to fix. However, the auditee may be asked to provide periodic status reports on the corrective action.

Corrective action must be effective. An auditor must verify that the proposed corrective action will prevent the identified problem and will not cause new problems.

Corrective action also must be preventive. It must identify and address a root cause in order to prevent the identified problem in the future.

STRATEGIES FOR VERIFYING CORRECTIVE ACTION

A review of the corrective action response and its timeliness is, in some instances, all the follow-up action that is necessary. This review, however, may indicate that the auditee is not responsive, is evasive, or that the proposed action is inadequate. When a response is questionable or unacceptable, the auditor should immediately contact the auditee to resolve the auditor's perception. A simple telephone call could alleviate the auditor's concern by clarifying the corrective action plan. The auditee's plan should be accepted, though, if there is a reasonable chance that it will correct the problem and preclude a recurrence; the auditor's way is not the only way.[4]

The auditor may have to return to the work area, observe the new process, ensure that the paperwork has been done, and ensure that employees have been trained in the new method; or verification can be as simple as reviewing paperwork. Closeout requires an actual verification activity.

Any action an auditee takes must be in agreement with the specified standard. The auditor's evaluation should be documented to ensure that all findings on the corrective action request have been addressed. The auditor records actions taken to verify the corrective action and the results of that verification. The auditee's action must be traceable to facilitate verification.

Auditors look for effectiveness, when required to do so by a client, to see if what the auditee is doing achieves the desired results. A performance-based auditing approach encourages one to examine additional criteria.

Chapter 19

Closure

Closure involves closing an audit after corrective action has been received, accepted, and verified. After notifying the auditee of the closure, the auditor may discard certain papers accumulated during an audit, but may be required to retain other records for specific time periods.

CRITERIA FOR CLOSURE

A letter of closure assessing the auditee's corrective action plan may be submitted to the client and/or auditee as applicable. This letter formally closes the audit.[1]

If a client is involved, communication between an auditor and auditee will usually go through the client, since the client is the main link with the audited organization. For an external audit, the contract may specify a contact person. Internally, audit reports go to a manager or possibly the audit manager and directly to the audited organization. A summary report of all audits performed goes to upper-level managers.

Sometimes each corrective action request is individually tracked. Tracking each item on the nonconformance report as an individual item instead of tracking the audit as a whole makes it possible to close out portions of an audit as applicable.

Upon resolution of each finding, written notification should be sent to those who received a copy of the initial report. This written notification not only satisfies the auditing department's records, but also lets the auditee know that the corrective actions have been accepted. If a satisfactory resolution cannot be reached with the auditee, the finding should be forwarded to upper management for resolution and then closed out if so directed.

CRITERIA FOR RECORD RETENTION

All audit documents are retained by the auditing organization or are retained by agreement between the client, the auditing organization, and the auditee, or in accordance with any regulatory requirements. Auditors should adopt reasonable procedures to ensure the safe custody and retention of working papers for a period of time sufficient to satisfy pertinent legal and administrative requirements.[2]

Properly retained documents of an audit—working papers and reports—facilitate future audit planning, review of audit work, preparation of reports on the work of audit departments/groups, and proof of compliance with audit standards. Complete reports, including supplemental documents, should be retained at least until the next formal audit is complete, as evidence that the findings of an earlier audit have been identified, corrected, and maintained.[3]

Audit records are maintained primarily as evidence that the quality program has been evaluated; and secondarily that the audits were planned, conducted, and reported according to established procedures. Included in the category of quality records of the audit system are audit schedules, audit plans, audit reports, completed audit checklists, auditor qualification records, and audit follow-up records.[4]

Audit records may be classified as either long-term or short-term records, depending upon their use and the length of time they are kept.[5]

Long-Term Records

While practices vary, five years is considered a good length of time to keep long-term records. Auditors in regulated industries, such as pharmaceuticals or nuclear power, should check with their legal staffs or contract administrators.[6] Examples of long-term records include the following:

- Audit notification letter and audit plan
- Blank checklists
- Audit report and cover letter
- Response from the auditee
- Follow-up audit or verification results
- Closing letter

Short-Term Records

Short-term records are kept mainly for an auditor's own use—not to document audit procedures. A good length of time to keep these records is one year, or until the next audit of that area.[7] Short-term records include the following:

- Copies of auditor qualification records
- Completed checklists (working papers)
- Documents and records obtained from the auditee
- Additional correspondence

The organization responsible for conducting and reporting audits should maintain the original supporting records generated during the audit and used to prepare the final report. These papers are temporary or working records that should be maintained for one to two years or until the completion of the next audit.[8]

In all cases, official audit records and documents to be retained should be labeled. The retention time for the audit files should be consistent with organization policy and legal requirements.

Problems Commonly Encountered During the Audit Reporting and Closure Stage

The following are examples of the types of problems commonly encountered during the audit reporting and closure stage.

Lack of Response or Inadequate Response. Sometimes an auditee will fail to take the action specified on the corrective action plan. The auditee may fail to notify the auditing organization when they do take action, or the action taken may not be sufficient to warrant closing out the finding. The auditee may lose sight of the original intent of the corrective action request and address a different issue. At times, an auditee simply may not understand what a standard says or means and may argue the issue's importance or relevance. As a result, an auditee may try to fix a problem haphazardly without understanding the need for remedial action or training. Sometimes the person involved in fixing a problem was not involved in the audit and may not have all of the needed information. An auditee may try to pit one audit team against another and argue that the other audit team had no findings in a certain area.

Continual Requests for Extensions. Sometimes an auditor and auditee may not agree on the significance of a problem. When vested interest is not the same, agreement on the importance or priority of solving a problem may be difficult to achieve. An auditee may request continual extensions for fixing the problem. Excuses can range from "We're working on a big order right now and don't have time to fix it right now" to "We forgot."

Part V

Auditing Tools and Techniques

Chapter 20
Auditing Techniques

An auditor must understand the techniques used when observing work in process and physically examining items, as well as sampling theory and procedures. Additionally, an auditor should follow certain guidelines for making presentations and managing time.

The following discussions highlight those techniques that auditors find to be most effective for gathering information during an audit. (One important technique, interviewing, is discussed in Chapter 14.) All of these auditing techniques are important and should be used in combination as appropriate to perform effective audits.

Before deciding what techniques or tools are applicable during a specific audit, an auditor must understand the business to be audited and establish communication with the auditee. No information-gathering technique can compensate for knowledge of and ability to communicate with an auditee.

OBSERVATION TECHNIQUES

An auditor observes work in process to see if it meets requirements. An auditor gains this knowledge by monitoring a process being performed to see how the work is being done. Many of the interviewing techniques discussed earlier in this handbook also apply to observation.

Observation means "to watch attentively" or "to watch or be present without participating actively." Hence, auditors must be well-trained in observation techniques so that they learn *how* to observe closely, but not obtrusively. An auditor's presence may be distracting to people at work; therefore, an auditor needs to minimize any interference resulting from it. An auditor also should realize that sometimes disrupting a worker may be unsafe.

An auditor also needs to know *when* to observe work. For example, where shift changes are involved, the auditor may desire to observe work being performed by different shifts. An auditor also should be aware of when shift changes will be taking place or when employees' breaks are approaching to avoid retaining people through shift changes or during breaks.

Most importantly, auditors need to understand *what* to observe and, after observing, what they have seen. The characteristics observed often include some of the causal factors discussed on pages 158–161 of this handbook.

- *Product.* The auditor should establish if the product is made according to the documented procedures by the individuals responsible for using the specified equipment. The auditor records the results of observations.

- *Equipment.* When looking at equipment, the auditor should note the type, condition, use, and any identification tags or numbers. The auditor also should establish that the equipment has been properly maintained and calibrated, if applicable.

- *Individuals.* The auditor should verify that employees are familiar with policies and procedures; that they know their responsibilities and roles; and that they have the necessary training, skills, experience, and authority to perform their jobs.

- *Documents.* When reviewing documents, an auditor should verify certain characteristics: contents, type, scope, format, readability, and date, for example. How the document has been filed and distributed and the method by which any modifications have been made are also important.

By listening and watching, an auditor should be able to ascertain if what the worker is doing supports the procedures outlined in quality-related documentation. It is usually best if an auditor observes people doing their actual work rather than creating work for them.

PHYSICAL EXAMINATION TOOLS AND TECHNIQUES

The types of physical examination tools used by auditors can vary widely depending on the industry. An auditor needs to be familiar with the tools and techniques applicable to the industry or company being audited. In addition to knowing which tool to use in what situation, the auditor should be aware of the problems that can arise if tools are used incorrectly or inconsistently. If the auditor has no experience with the necessary tools, a technical expert should be included as part of the audit team.

Physical examination tools are normally associated with product audits. In a heavy manufacturing environment an auditor may use calipers, steel rules, or micrometers, for example, to take measurements. An auditor may also observe others using these tools in order to verify that a product meets certain characteristics. In most circumstances it is essential that tools have been properly calibrated. However, exceptions do exist. For example, a volt meter may be used to determine if power is turned on or off, not to measure voltage. If the auditor uses measuring devices that need calibrating, the auditing organization should follow an accepted calibration program.

PRESENTATION METHODS AND TECHNIQUES

Members of an audit team must create a favorable impression to auditee management, both in appearance and ability. Audit team members should dress appropriately for the opening meeting. Credentials of the audit team members are also presented at this time to instill auditee management with confidence that the audit is being performed by competent, well-qualified individuals.

The lead auditor conducts the opening and closing meetings, as well as separate daily meetings with the auditee and the audit team. By using appropriate aids and handouts, the lead auditor ensures that the auditee is in agreement with the details outlined in the audit plan and understands the auditing method(s) to be used. In addition, the auditor should ensure that the auditee is able to interpret data correctly, is in accord with the information presented on the audit report, and desires to implement the needed corrective action.

Some auditing organizations prefer that audit team members sit together during meetings, with auditee representatives likewise grouped. They believe that such an arrangement shows cohesion and support for one another. Other auditing organizations favor a less formal atmosphere, with auditors and auditees intermingled.

Regardless of the approach favored, the lead auditor should be certain to communicate the data analysis to the auditee both orally and visually. Using simple statistical techniques to recognize patterns and trends and evaluate their significance enables an auditor to prepare an audit report. These results must be communicated to the auditee in a timely and effective manner, and the inclusion of simple charts or graphs in the audit report or their display on an overhead projector can assist the auditee in gaining the necessary understanding of a problem.

TIME MANAGEMENT TECHNIQUES

Proper preparation in the audit planning stage can eliminate many delays in the audit performance stage. To make the most efficient use of time, the auditor must plan an audit on several levels. First, the audit manager must schedule each individual audit in relation to other audits being performed so that availability of audit team members and other resources can be assessed. Next, the lead auditor must prepare the audit plan for the individual audit. The steps involved in this audit phase are discussed in Part II of this handbook. Once a lead auditor establishes the auditing strategy, he or she must prepare a detailed schedule that specifies which areas are to be visited at various times throughout the day. The detailed schedule may be revised constantly throughout the audit, but the auditor must inform auditee management about planned activities. An auditor who makes no attempt to stick to the proposed plan may antagonize members of the auditee's organization who have made arrangements to be available as requested.

The auditor's notification letter to the auditee should specify any special arrangements that need to be made, such as transportation from one audit site to another, the need for an escort, use of special safety equipment, or the need for a conference room. At this time the auditor also should list required equipment or supplies, such as access to copy machines or printers, overhead projectors, and extension cords. By anticipating needs and making them known to the auditee in advance, an auditor communicates preparedness and a strong desire to focus on the important task of information gathering at the audit site.

To ensure the efficient use of time during the audit performance stage, the audit team should arrive promptly at the audit site at the agreed-on time for the opening meeting. The lead auditor should retain control of the opening meeting and should not allow the auditee to gain control with extended plant tours or lengthy presentations, unless such time has been scheduled into the audit.

Throughout an audit, the audit team meets daily to assess audit progress. Additionally, auditors should allow several minutes at the end of each interview to review notes, present conclusions, and reach a consensus with an auditee representative, for example, the area supervisor or escort. If data indicate that certain areas need additional attention, the auditors' assignments may need to be changed. Findings that may indicate severe ramifications for the quality program should be investigated thoroughly as soon as they are uncovered, while the investigation of less critical observations may be saved for the end of the audit.

Audit teams often ask to have lunch catered so that a working lunch can take place. Scheduling a small amount of time for an audit team meeting during the lunch break may aid the auditors in gathering additional information if needed. An audit team should allow sufficient time to prepare for the closing meeting. Especially in the case of an audit that is several days long, extra time at the end of the audit is often a good idea in case additional information needs to be gathered.

An auditor should be able to recognize and overcome delay tactics. Common time-wasting techniques employed by auditees and possible solutions by auditors are discussed in Figure 2.2 (page 36). When an auditee's repeated time-wasting tactics hinder the progress of an audit and threaten to compromise the audit schedule severely, the lead auditor is responsible for notifying auditee management.

SAMPLING THEORY AND PROCEDURES

Sampling is a practice of taking selected items or units from a total population of items or units. The method and reason for taking certain samples or number of samples from a population should be based on sampling theory and procedures. Samples may be taken from the total population, or *universe;* or the population may be separated into subgroups called *strata*. Inferences drawn from the sampling of a strata, however, are not valid for the total population.

To infer statistical significance from any sample, two conditions must be met. The population under consideration must be homogeneous and the sample must be random. *Homogeneous* means that the population must be uniform throughout—the bad parts should not be hidden on the bottom of one load—or it could refer to the similarities that should exist when one load is checked against others from a different production setup. *Random* means that every item in the population has an equal chance of being checked. To ensure this, samples can be pulled by a random number generator or other unbiased method.

The sampling process must be correct to avoid making incorrect assumptions. Proper consideration must be given to sample size, sample amount, location of samples, and sampling errors.[1]

Auditors should not waste time sampling in areas that are not important. For example, when auditing a medical device supplier, an auditor's sampling is dictated by the potential impact or severity of a failure in the device or service that is being observed. Sampling should be weighted toward critical suppliers of pacemakers as opposed to those of bed pans or tongue depressors.

When looking at records, an auditor should take care not to pull all of the samples out of one file drawer or from just the front or back of drawers. Lower drawers are typically more neglected than other drawers. If files are color coded, the auditor should ask what the color codes mean and choose samples from each set.

An auditor may choose samples on the basis of previous audit results. In addition, an auditor should verify in each audit that problems detected by previous audits have remained corrected. Also, if any major changes have been made to a system (for example, calibration once done in-house is now done outside), the auditor may desire to pull a larger-than-usual sample.

It is preferable for the auditor to go to the location of the sample and then select the sample for the audit. However, there are situations (long distances, convenience, files off site) where it is permissible for the auditee to provide the sample population—such as in a file, folder, or log book—to the auditor, who can then select the sample.

Chapter 21
Auditing Tools

Auditing tools, also called quality tools, can be used by an auditor or auditee. An auditor uses many types of tools to plan and perform an audit, as well as to analyze and report the results. The auditor or auditee may use the same or similar tools to prioritize problems and to evaluate the actual or potential results of a corrective action plan.

With data portrayed in the form of charts and graphs, an auditor and auditee gain a greater understanding of the steps involved in solving problems, maintaining controls, and achieving improvements in systems, processes, and products.[1]

Additionally, the auditor should be experienced in using these tools to analyze patterns and trends and to distinguish between symptoms and root causes of problems. Only by collecting representative data and interpreting them correctly through the use of descriptive statistics can the auditor assist the auditee in implementing or evaluating effective and preventive measures that ensure continuous improvement.

An auditor must have sufficient knowledge of quality tools to evaluate if the auditee is using these tools correctly and effectively. Besides understanding how to use and interpret these tools, an auditor must understand the limitations of such tools. For more in-depth information on the application of these tools or others not included here, readers should consult an appropriate textbook.

DATA AND DATA COLLECTION

Data consist of facts gathered through some established information collection method. Quality auditing is an information-intensive activity: Auditors need clear, useful information to make effective auditing judgments and decisions. Information must be based on data (facts), but merely obtaining data does not guarantee that the information will be useful. To collect data successfully, an auditor must know what question to ask and then collect, process, analyze, and present the specific data needed to answer that question.[2]

The use of quality tools depends on reliable, accurate data. If such data are not available, the data must be collected. The data collection process must focus on getting informative answers to questions based on information needs. Data must be validated and guarded against possible biases. Careful planning and design of the collection process will avoid or reduce the impact of potential sources of biases.[3]

The most commonly used data collection forms include check sheets and data sheets. A check sheet is a simple data-recording form that has been specially designed so that the results can be readily interpreted from the form itself. Data sheets differ from check sheets in that the data are recorded in a tabular or columnar format. Additional processing (grouping, calculating) typically is required before an analysis tool is applied to the data. Data can be variable or attribute.

Variable Data

Variable data, also called *continuous data* or *measurement data,* are collected from measurements of the items being evaluated. For example, the measurement of physical characteristics such as time, length, weight, pressure, or volume through inspection, testing, or measuring equipment constitutes variable data collection. Variable data can be measured and plotted on a continuous scale and are often expressed as fractions or decimals.

Because the collection of variable data may involve much time and the use of meticulous measurements, it is generally difficult and expensive. However, variable data usually provide more information than attribute data.

Attribute Data

Attribute data, also referred to as *discrete data* or *counted data,* provide information on number and frequency of occurrence. By counting and plotting discrete events—the number of defects or percentage of failures, for example—in integer values (1, 2, 3, etc.), an auditor is able to look at previously defined criteria and rate the product or system as pass/fail, acceptable/unacceptable, or go/no-go.

Generally it is less difficult and less expensive to collect attribute data, but they also provide less information than variable data.

See the "Control Charts" section later in this chapter for more information on variable and attribute data.

TYPES OF CHARTS AND GRAPHS

Charts and graphs are visual representations of data made up of points, lines, geometric shapes, letters, words, numbers, shades, and colors. They are used to summarize large amounts of information in a small area and to communicate complex situations concisely and clearly.[4]

Many types of charts and graphs exist. Commonly used charts or graphs in auditing include: line graphs, bar graphs, pie charts, flowcharts and process maps, Pareto charts, cause-and-effect diagrams, control charts, and histograms.

When constructing graphs and charts, the following concepts need to be kept in mind: graphic integrity, scale and symbol consistency, readability, and simplicity.

Line Graphs

Line graphs connect points, which represent pairs of numeric data, to show how one variable of the pair is a function of the other. As a matter of convention, independent variables are plotted on the horizontal axis and dependent variables are plotted on the vertical axis. Line graphs show *trends.*[5] A line graph is shown in Figure 21.1.[6]

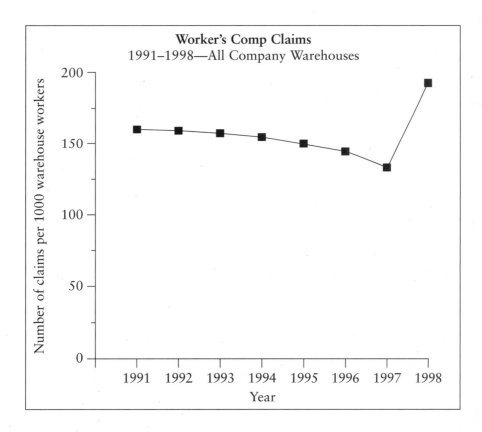

Figure 21.1. Line graph.

Bar Graphs

Bar graphs also portray the relationship or comparison between pairs of variables, but one of the variables need not be numeric. Each bar in a bar graph represents a separate, or discrete, value. Bar graphs show *relationships* or *comparisons.*[7] A bar graph is shown in Figure 21.2.[8]

Pie Charts

Pie charts depict proportions of the various classes of phenomenon being studied that make up the whole. The entire circle, or *pie,* represents 100 percent of the data. The circle is divided into "slices," with each segment proportional to the numeric quantity in each class or category. Pie charts show *proportions.*[9] A pie chart is shown in Figure 21.3.[10]

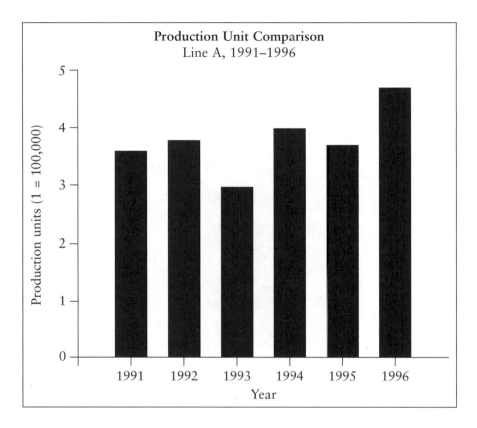

Figure 21.2. Bar graph.

Flowcharts/Process Maps/Tree Diagrams

Before taking action on a process, an individual must first understand exactly how the process works. The easiest and best way to understand a process is to draw a picture of it.[11] Flowcharts, process maps, and tree diagrams are three tools to do this.

Flowcharts. Flowcharts, or flow diagrams, depict the sequence of steps or events in a process or system that produces some output. Flowcharts are an effective means for understanding procedures and overall processes of an organization. Flowcharts are especially helpful in understanding processes that are complicated or that appear to be disordered. Auditors can flowchart both production and service processes.

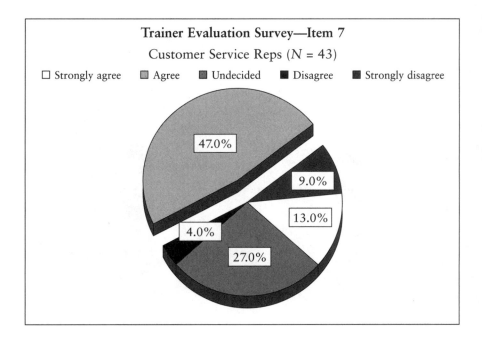

Figure 21.3. Pie chart.

A flowchart can be used to describe an existing system or process or to design a new one. A flowchart can be used to

- Develop a common understanding of an overall process or system and sequence of operations.

- Identify potential problem areas, bottlenecks, unnecessary steps or loops, and rework loops.

- Discover opportunities for changes and improvements.

- Guide activities for identifying problems, theorizing about root causes, developing potential corrective actions and solutions, and achieving continuous improvement.[12]

Flowcharting usually follows a sequence from top to bottom and left to right, with arrowheads used to indicate the directions of the flows. Flowcharting symbols are standardized, but how they are standardized depends on the discipline and use of the symbols. Templates or computer software are available for drawing them. Commonly used symbols often used in quality applications are shown below. However, there are many other types of symbols used in flowcharting, and there are standards for flowcharting such as ANSI Y 15.3, *Operation and Flow Process Charts.*

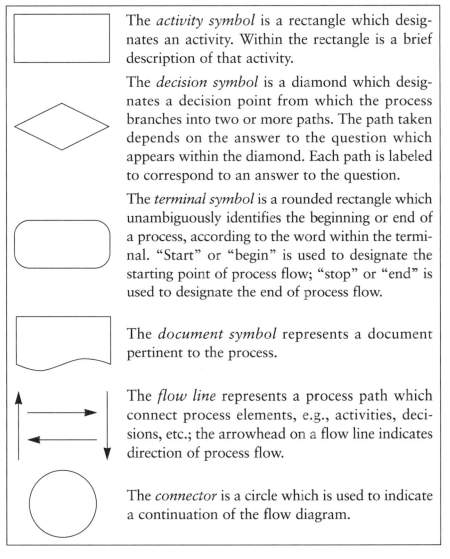

The *activity symbol* is a rectangle which designates an activity. Within the rectangle is a brief description of that activity.

The *decision symbol* is a diamond which designates a decision point from which the process branches into two or more paths. The path taken depends on the answer to the question which appears within the diamond. Each path is labeled to correspond to an answer to the question.

The *terminal symbol* is a rounded rectangle which unambiguously identifies the beginning or end of a process, according to the word within the terminal. "Start" or "begin" is used to designate the starting point of process flow; "stop" or "end" is used to designate the end of process flow.

The *document symbol* represents a document pertinent to the process.

The *flow line* represents a process path which connect process elements, e.g., activities, decisions, etc.; the arrowhead on a flow line indicates direction of process flow.

The *connector* is a circle which is used to indicate a continuation of the flow diagram.

Source: J. M. Juran, ed., *Juran's Quality Control Handbook,* 4th ed. (New York: McGraw-Hill, 1988), p. 67. Reproduced with permission of The McGraw-Hill Companies.

Figure 21.4a[13] shows a process flowchart for a design project. Other uses of flowcharting techniques include those shown in Figure 21.4b through 21.4d.

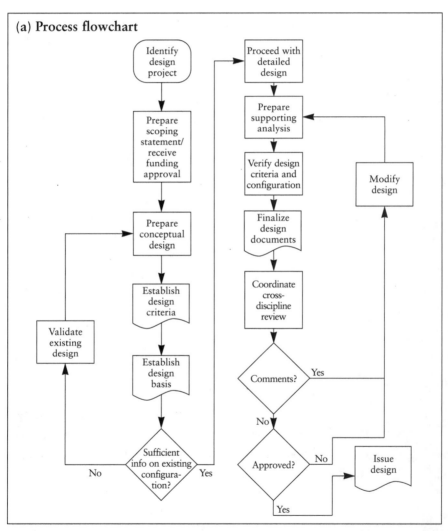

(a) Process flowchart

Source: Rudolph C. Hirzel, "Audits Making a Difference" (presented at the ASQC Fifth Annual Quality Audit Conference, 22-23 February 1996, Kansas City, Missouri). Used with permission.

Figure 21.4. Type of flowcharts.

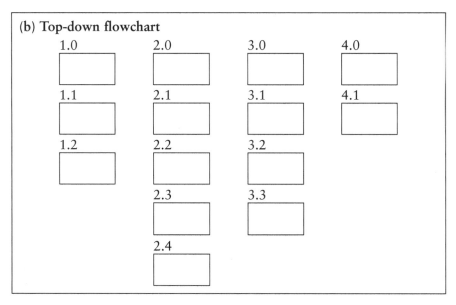

Figures 21.4(b)-(d) *Source:* Entner, Dan, "Basic Tools for Process Improvement." Unpublished paper, Delaware Community College. Used with permission.

Figure 21.4.

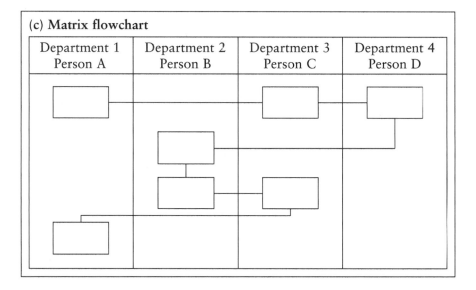

Figure 21.4. *Continued.*

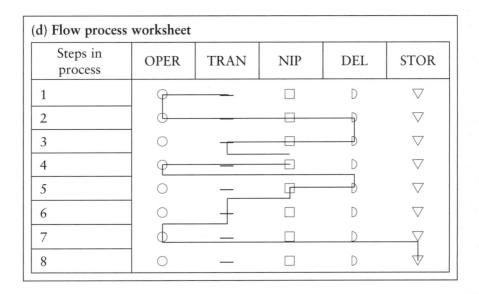

Figure 21.4. *Continued.*

Process Maps. A process map is similar to a flowchart. It is defined as "a graphic representation of a process, showing the sequence of tasks; uses a modified version of standard flowcharting symbols."[14] Mapping is the activity of creating a detailed flowchart of a work process showing its inputs, tasks, and activities in sequence. A process map may provide a broader perspective than typical flowcharts.

Tree Diagrams. A tree diagram is a graphical representation of the major components of a selected subject, program, or criterion. As with flowcharts, tree diagram components—which are intended to depict an element of a system—flow down from a main heading. The tree diagram developed by one company to evaluate the effectiveness of its suppliers' quality programs is shown in Figure 21.5.[15] In this example, the tree diagram can be thought of as layers of audit questions, similar to those contained in a checklist. For instance, the following questions are some of many that could be developed from Figure 21.5.

- Does a *program* exist for quality assurance?
- Does the program contain *performance objectives*?

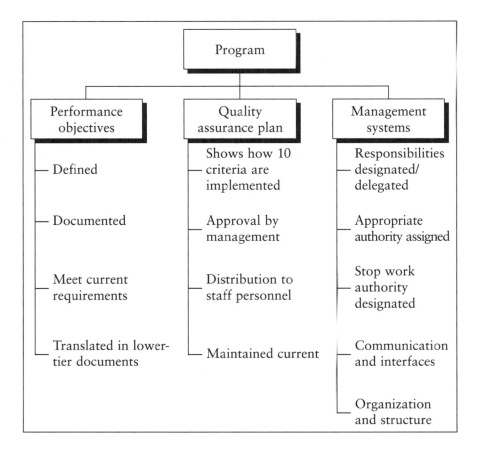

Figure 21.5. Tree diagram.

- Are the performance objectives *defined* in the program?

- Are these performance objectives *documented*?

- Do the documented performance objectives defined by the quality assurance program *meet current requirements*?

By condensing components of the system or process visually onto one page, the tree diagram assists the auditor and auditee in determining and understanding what will be examined during the audit. In addition, individual elements for each criterion can be coded, allowing for the tracking of audit results.

Many benefits can result from the use of this quality tool in auditing. Tree diagrams

- Are an excellent tool for planning audit performance and tracking audit results.

- Are useful for communicating quality program expectations/requirements to the auditee.

- Are very flexible; they can be applied to a wide range of activities and facilities.

- Provide a general map of what needs to be audited; they also ensure consistency and permit detailed application.

- Can foster better dialogue during individual interviews. For example, the auditor may say, "Tell me how you accomplish these elements and it will help me understand how you meet the criterion."[16]

Pareto Charts

Pareto charts, also called Pareto diagrams or Pareto analysis, are based on the Pareto principle, which suggests that most effects come from relatively few causes. As shown in Figure 21.6, a Pareto chart consists of a series of bars in descending order. The bars with the highest incidence, failures, costs, or other occurrences are on the left side. The miscellaneous category, an exception, always appears at the far right, regardless of size. Pareto charts display, in order of importance, the contribution of each item to the total effect and the relative rank of the items.

Pareto charts can be used to prioritize problems and to check performance of implemented solutions to problems. The Pareto chart can be a powerful management tool for focusing effort on the problems and solutions that have the greatest payback.[17] Some organizations construct Paretos at year end and form corporate quality improvement teams in the areas determined to be in need of the greatest attention.

Cause-and-Effect Diagrams

The cause-and-effect diagram (C-E diagram) is a visual method for analyzing causal factors of process dispersion (a process being any set

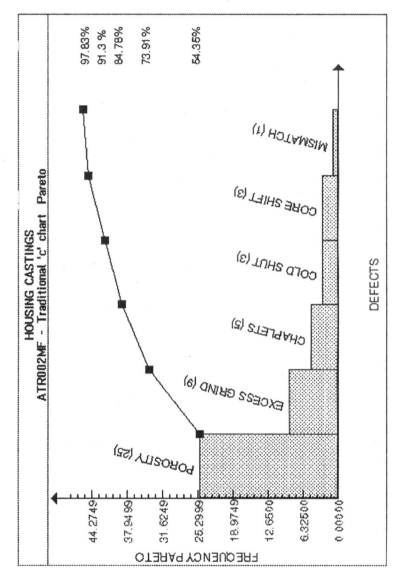

Courtesy of CIM Vision International.

Figure 21.6. SQM software example of a frequency Pareto analysis.

of interrelated resources and activities that transforms inputs to outputs). The diagram's purpose is to relate causes and effects.[18] The diagram is also called an Ishikawa diagram after its inventor, or a fishbone diagram because of its shape.

One of the most widely used quality tools, the C-E diagram provides an excellent means to facilitate a brainstorming session. It allows participants to focus on the issue at hand and sort ideas into useful categories.[19]

Prominent basic features of this tool include the following: (1) It represents the factors that might contribute to an observed phenomena or effect that is being examined; (2) it clearly shows interrelationships among possible causal factors; and (3) the interrelationships shown are usually based on known data collected during the audit. C-E diagrams are an effective way to generate and organize theories about root causes of observed phenomena, since they help individuals be systematic in the generation of theories and in checking that the stated direction of causation has been correctly identified.[20]

C-E diagrams illustrate the relationship between a known "effect" or outcome and all the possible "causes" or contributors influencing it. The effect being examined may represent either a wanted or unwanted outcome. Figure 21.7 is a C-E diagram used to identify all of the program elements that should be in place to prevent worker exposure to hazards.[21] The problem or process constituting the effect—"prevent worker exposure"—is named in the head of the "fishbone." Ideas about the causes of the effect are identified in the major identifiable branches. These main branches are some of the typical groupings of causal factors of dispersion.

- People (worker) influences
- Equipment (machine) influences
- Method influences
- Material influences
- Environmental influences
- Measurement influences

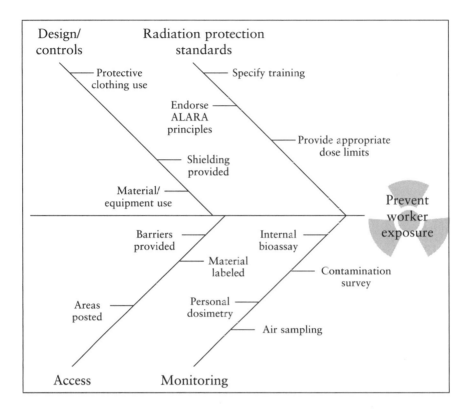

Figure 21.7. Cause-and-effect diagram.

In a C-E diagram, each of these categories is further subdivided as possible problems are suggested. The C-E diagram does not provide solutions to problems. It serves as a vehicle for producing all known or suspected causes that potentially contribute to an observed effect. Other tools must be used to analyze real data, since the C-E diagram simply arranges theories.[22]

Histograms and Frequency Distributions

A histogram is a graphic summary of variation in a set of data. Histograms, such as the one shown in Figure 21.8, give a clearer and more complete picture of the data than would a table of numbers since patterns may be difficult to discern in a table. Patterns of variation in

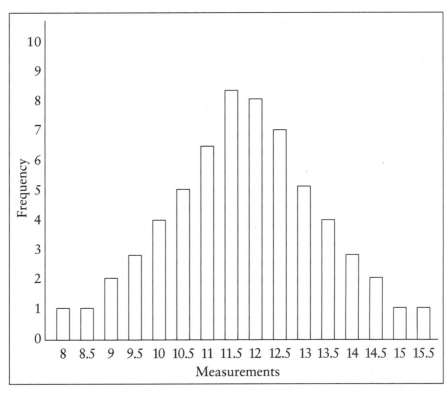

Source: Gary K. Griffith, *Statistical Process Control Methods for Long and Short Runs,* 2d ed. (Milwaukee: ASQC Quality Press, 1995), p. 195. Used with permission.

Figure 21.8. Histogram with normal distribution.

data are called distributions. Often identifiable patterns exist in the variation, and the correct interpretation of these patterns can help to identify the cause of a problem. The histogram is a useful tool when a team is faced with the task of analyzing data that contain variation.[23]

The histogram is used to highlight the center and the amount of variation in a sample of data. It provides a vertical bar chart of a frequency distribution. The histogram's simplicity of construction and interpretation makes it an effective tool in the quality auditor's elementary analysis of collected data. A histogram is one of the simplest procedures for organizing and summarizing data. It is an arrangement of values that shows the number of times that a given score or group of scores occurs.

The following are key concepts about data.

- Values in a set of data almost always show variation.

- Variation displays a pattern.

- Patterns of variation are difficult to see in a table of numbers.

- Patterns are easier to see pictorially in a histogram.[24]

The histogram is not sensitive enough to allow firm conclusions about small differences in variability or in the locations of peaks in distributions. This fact is especially true when the sample size is small. Confidence intervals, hypothesis tests, analysis of means, and analysis of variance are the proper tools for these situations.[25]

Histograms should indicate sample size to communicate the degree of confidence in the conclusions. Once a histogram has been completed, it should be analyzed by (1) identifying and classifying the pattern of variation and (2) developing a plausible and relevant explanation for the pattern.[26] For a normal distribution, the following identifiable patterns, shown in Figure 21.9, are commonly observed in histograms.

a. *Bell-shaped*. A symmetrical shape with a peak in the middle of the range of data. This is the normal and natural distribution of data. Deviations from the bell shape might indicate the presence of complicating factors or outside influences. While deviations from a bell shape should be investigated, such deviations are not necessarily bad.

b. *Double-peaked (bimodal)*. A distinct valley in the middle of the range of the data with peaks on either side. Usually a combination of two bell-shaped distributions, this pattern indicates that two distinct processes are causing this distribution.

c. *Plateau*. A flat top with no distinct peak and slight tails on either side. This pattern is likely to be the result of many different bell-shaped distributions with centers spread evenly throughout the range of data.

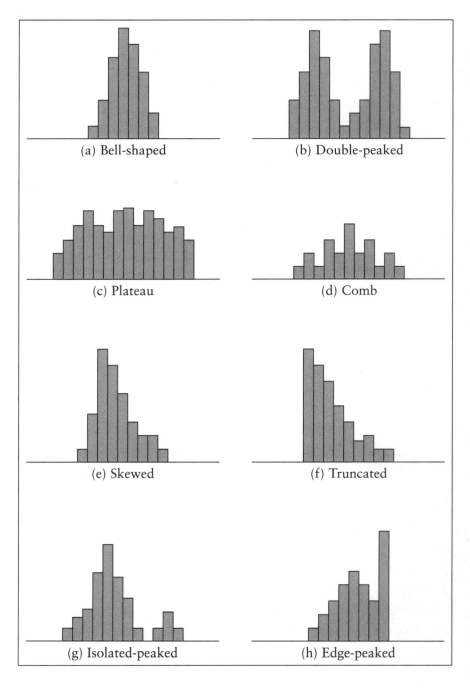

Figure 21.9. Common histogram patterns.

d. *Comb.* High and low values alternating in a regular fashion. This pattern typically indicates measurement error, errors in the way data were grouped to construct the histogram, or a systematic bias in the way data were rounded off. A less likely alternative is that this is a type of plateau distribution.

e. *Skewed.* An asymmetrical shape in which the peak is off-center in the range of data and the distribution tails off sharply on one side and gently on the other. If the long tail extends rightward, toward increasing values, the distribution is positively skewed; a negatively skewed distribution exists when the long tail extends leftward, toward decreasing values. The skewed pattern typically occurs when a practical limit, or a specification limit, exists on one side and is relatively close to the nominal value. In this case, there simply are not as many values available on the one side as on the other.

f. *Truncated.* An asymmetrical shape in which the peak is at or near the edge of the range of the data, and the distribution ends very abruptly on one side and tails off gently on the other. Truncated distributions are often smooth, bell-shaped distributions with a part of the distribution removed, or truncated, by some external force.

g. *Isolated-peaked.* A small, separate group of data in addition to the larger distribution. Similar to the double-peaked distribution; however, the short bell shape indicates something that doesn't happen very often.

h. *Edge-peaked.* A large peak is appended to an otherwise smooth distribution. Similar to the comb distribution in that an error was probably made in the data. All readings past a certain point may have been grouped into one value.[27]

No rules exist to explain pattern variation in every situation. Explanations must be based on knowledge and observation of the specific situation and confirmed through additional analysis. The histogram is used to understand the process and develop plausible, fact-based theories about the root causes of problems. Depending on what is being measured and what values the histogram represents, consideration should be given to the possibility that the distribution may not be normal and the data may actually be distributed according to some other distribution such as exponential, gamma, uniform, etc. Analysis of distributions of these types is beyond the scope of this text, and further information should be sought from specialized statistics texts. The pattern of variation often leads to stratification (breaking up) of data in various ways to discover additional patterns. Histograms can also be used to indicate that problems have been solved—that is, that causes have been eliminated.[28]

The three most important characteristics of histograms are centering (central tendency), width (spread, variation, scatter, dispersion, etc.), and shape (pattern). If no discernible pattern appears to exist, data should be regrouped (using the process known as stratification) and analyzed again.

Control Charts

Many companies use statistical process control (SPC) techniques as part of a continuing quality improvement effort. Quality auditors should be familiar with statistical techniques so that they can evaluate whether they are being properly applied by the company being audited.[29] Control charts, also called process control charts or run charts, are a method of SPC.

SPC uses statistics to tell the operator when to adjust a process and when to leave it alone. SPC recognizes that some random variation always exists and is a tool to control distribution rather than the individual dimensions. The ability to operate to a tight tolerance without producing defects can be a major business advantage. Control charts can tell an organization when a process is good enough so that improvement resources can be directed to more pressing needs.[30]

A control chart, such as the one shown in Figure 21.10, is used for distinguishing variations in a process over time. Variations can be attributed to either special or common causes. Common-cause variations repeat randomly within predictable limits and can include chance causes, random causes, system causes, and inherent causes. Special cause variations indicate that some factors affecting the process need to be identified, investigated, and brought under control. Such causes include assignable causes, local causes, and specific causes. Control charts use operating data to establish limits within

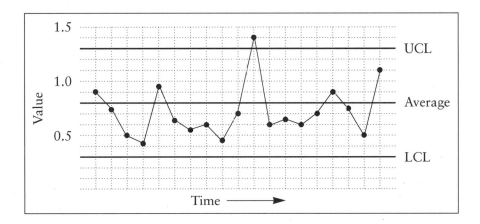

Source: Nancy R. Tague, *The Quality Toolbox* (Milwaukee: ASQC Quality Press, 1995), p. 86. Used with permission.

Figure 21.10. Control chart.

which future observations are expected to remain if the process remains unaffected by special causes.[31]

"Control charts can monitor the aim and variability, and thereby continually check the stability, of a process. This check of stability in turn ensures that the statistical distribution of the product characteristic is consistent with quality requirements."[32]

"Control charts are commonly used to:

1. Attain a state of statistical control

2. Monitor a process

3. Determine process capability"[33]

The type of control chart to be used in a specific situation depends on the type of data being measured or counted.

For Variable Data. The $\overline{X}$ (average) chart and the R (range) chart are the most common types of control charts for variable data. The $\overline{X}$ control chart illustrates the average measurement of samples taken over time. The R control chart illustrates the range of the measurements of the samples taken. For these charts to be accurate, it is critical that individual items comprising the sample are pulled from the same basic production process. That is, the samples should be drawn around the same time, from the same machine, from the same raw material source, etc.[34] These charts are often used in conjunction with one another to record jointly the mean and range of samples taken from the process at fairly regular intervals. Figure 21.11 shows an $\bar{X}$–R chart.

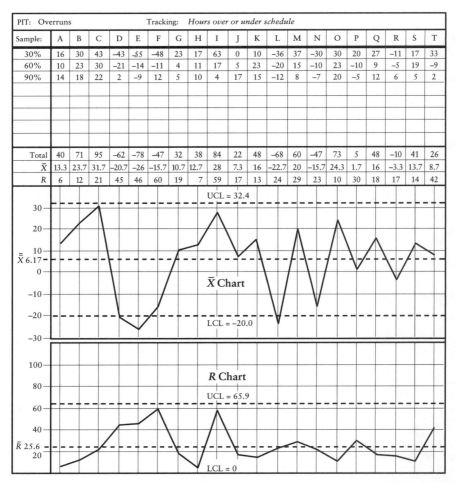

PIT: Overruns							Tracking:	*Hours over or under schedule*											
Sample:	A	B	C	D	E	F	G	H	I	J	K	L	M	N	O	P	Q	R	S	T
30%	16	30	43	–43	–55	–48	23	17	63	0	10	–36	37	–30	30	20	27	–11	17	33
60%	10	23	30	–21	–14	–11	4	11	17	5	23	–20	15	–10	23	–10	9	–5	19	–9
90%	14	18	22	2	–9	12	5	10	4	17	15	–12	8	–7	20	–5	12	6	5	2
Total	40	71	95	–62	–78	–47	32	38	84	22	48	–68	60	–47	73	5	48	–10	41	26
$\bar{X}$	13.3	23.7	31.7	–20.7	–26	–15.7	10.7	12.7	28	7.3	16	–22.7	20	–15.7	24.3	1.7	16	–3.3	13.7	8.7
R	6	12	21	45	46	60	19	7	59	17	13	24	29	23	10	30	18	17	14	42

UCL = 32.4

$\bar{X}$ Chart

$\bar{\bar{X}}$ 6.17

LCL = –20.0

R Chart

UCL = 65.9

$\bar{R}$ 25.6

LCL = 0

Source: Clive Shearer, *Practical Continuous Improvement for Professional Services* (Milwaukee: ASQC Quality Press, 1994) p. 241. Used with permission.

Figure 21.11. $\bar{X}$ and R chart example.

For Attribute Data. Several basic types of control charts can be used for charting attribute data. Attribute data can be either a fraction non-conforming, or number of defects or nonconformities observed in the sample. To chart fraction of units defective, the *p* chart is used. The units are classified into one of two states, go/no-go, acceptable/unacceptable, conforming/nonconforming, yes/no, and so on. The sample size may be fixed or variable, which makes the technique very effective for statistically monitoring nontraditional processes such as percent on-time delivery. Note, however, that if sample size is variable, control limits must be calculated for each sample taken. The *np* chart is a chart that uses the number nonconforming units in a sample. The *np* chart is sometimes easier for personnel to use who are not trained in SPC. It is easier to understand this chart when the sample size is constant, but it can be variable like the *p* chart.

The *c* chart plots the number of nonconformities per some unit of measure. For example, the total number of nonconformities could be counted at a final inspection of a product and charted on a *c* chart. The number of nonconformities may be made up of several distinct defects, which might then be analyzed for improvement of the process. For this chart, the sample size must be constant for unit to unit.

The *u* chart is used for average number of nonconformities per some unit of measure. It can have either variable or constant samples size, since it is charting an average. A classic example is the number of nonconformities in a square yard of fabric in the textile industry. Bolts of cloth may vary in size, but an average can be calculated. Figure 21.12 shows an example of plotting attribute data using a *u* chart.

OTHER ANALYSIS TECHNIQUES

In conjunction with the quality tools mentioned, a quality auditor must have a grasp of several important methods in order to evaluate a quality system. Process capability, pattern and trend analysis, and root cause analysis are all concepts that an auditor must understand.

Process Capability

"One of the theories most widely encountered is: 'The process can't hold the tolerances.' To test this theory, measurements from the process

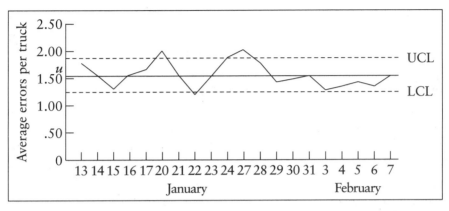

Source: John T. Burr, *SPC Tools for Everyone* (Milwaukee: ASQC Quality Press, 1993), p. 58. Used with permission.

Figure 21.12. *u* chart for the average errors per truck for 20 days of production.

must be taken and analyzed to determine the amount of variability inherent in the process. This variability is then compared to the specification limits. These steps are performed in a process-capability study."[35]

Process capability provides a quantified prediction of a process's adequacy and measures the capability of a process to produce products that meet specifications by measuring the inherent uniformity of the process. Generally, it is not feasible to determine process capability by direct measurement of a process under operating conditions, so capability is determined indirectly by measuring the uniformity of the product. Process capability can be used to measure process performance, monitor processes using control charts, evaluate process equipment, review tolerances based on common variation of a process, determine the effect of changes or adjustments to processes, and audit process performance.[36]

Process capability can be determined when a predictable pattern of statistically stable behavior consisting of common causes of variation are compared to specification limits. Process capability indices numerically express the relation between the distribution and the specification limits. A process is *in a state of statistical control* when the plotted data points are within the calculated upper control limit (UCL) and the lower control limit (LCL) almost all of the time (such as 99.73 percent) and the data do not display a particular form that would indicate an out-of-control condition (such as 7 successive data points below or above the center line of the control chart). A process is *capable* when the calculated UCL and LCL are within or equal to the upper specification limit (USL) and lower specification limit (LSL). Histograms can be used to graphically show capability when upper and lower control limits and specification limits are added to the histogram data.

A process capability index is a statistic that expresses a numerical relationship between the process variability and the specification limits. The most common indices currently in use are C_p and C_{pk}. If the upper control limit and lower control limit are superimposed upon the upper specification limit and lower specification limit, the C_p would equal 1. This assumes that the mean of the process is exactly on the target of the specification. If the control limits fall outside the specification limit, they would be greater than one. C_{pk} is a method of measuring process capability when the mean of the process is not on the target expressed by the specifications. A C_{pk} of 1 or greater means that the process is capable at a level of at least 99.73 percent conforming, which is the limit associated with an $\overline{X}$–R chart. It is extremely important when using these capability indices that the process be in control because the theory is based entirely on a normal distribution. If the distribution is not normal, the indices are meaningless.

Pattern and Trend Analysis

"Pattern analysis involves the collection of data in a way that readily reveals any kind of clustering that may occur. This technique is of major value in internal quality audits, since it is so effective in making use of data from repetitive audits. It can be both location- and time-sensitive. Pattern analysis is of limited value in external quality audits owing to the lack of repetition in such audits."[37] "A statistical control chart can be used to make visible trends in the performance data measured during the audit of a quality system. It can show this information in terms of both the average error rate and the acceptable performance level."[38]

While no one specific analytical tool exists to determine patterns and trends, the following tools—matrices and data systems—are among the many that can help to make such determinations. Patterns and trends often can indicate the severity of a problem—whether it goes from being a noncompliance to a systemic issue.

Matrices. Matrices are two-dimensional tables showing the relationship between two sets of information. They can be used to show the logical connecting points between performance criteria and implementing actions, or between required actions and personnel responsible for those actions. In this way, matrices are used to determine what actions and/or personnel have the greatest impact on an organization's mission. Matrices are especially useful as a way to focus auditing time and to organize auditing conduct.

In Table 21.1,[39] the matrix is used to help the auditor by identifying organizational responsibilities for the different audit areas. This particular matrix is used to maximize use of time during the site visit.

Table 21.2,[40] a much broader matrix, allows the auditor to do the long-range planning necessary for ensuring proper application of the audit program. In this example, the various audited areas (*y* axis) are applied against the different organizations to be audited.

Table 21.1. Area of responsibilities matrix.

	Program development	Deficiency tracking	Training	Work control	Documents and records retention	Assessment
Director		X				X
Ops office			X	X	X	
Ops support	X	X	X			
Tech support		X	X	X		X
Admin.			X		X	

Table 21.2. Audit planning matrix.

	Administration	Chemistry	Biology	Materials	Building services	Engineering
Industrial hygiene		A		A	A	A
Radiation protection	B		B	B		
Fire protection			C	C	C	C
Industrial safety	A	A			A	
Environmental	C	C	C			C
Personnel training	B	A		B		C
Conduct of ops			C	C	C	
Quality assurance		A	C		A	C

A = First assessment   B = Second assessment   C = Third assessment

Data Systems. Data systems exist in a wide range of forms and formats. They may include the weekly and monthly reports of laboratory or organizational performance that are used to alert the auditing organization of potential audit areas, or computerized databases that link performance to specific performance objectives or track actions to resolve programmatic weaknesses. In any case, data systems are an important tool that provides the auditor with the data needed to focus on audit activities.

In Table 21.3,[41] information on lost-time injuries is displayed in tabular form; the same information is displayed as a graph in Figure 21.13.[42] This information can be used to focus the assessment on either the location of the injuries or the work procedures involved to identify any weaknesses in the accident prevention program.

Table 21.3. Lost-time accident monthly summary.

Date	Type	Area	Work procedure	Work crew	Days lost
5/3	Sprain	Bldg 12	CAP-101	Mech	4
5/5	Sprain	Bldg 5	MAP-2-12	Elec	5
5/12	Burn	Area 8	PMP-1-4	Mech	2
5/15	Abrasion	Area 10	PMP-3-7	Grnds	3
5/23	Burn	Bldg 12	CAP-103	Elec	1
5/25	Sprain	Admin bldg	N/A	N/A	1
5/29	Cut	Bldg 5	MAP-2-17	Elec	1

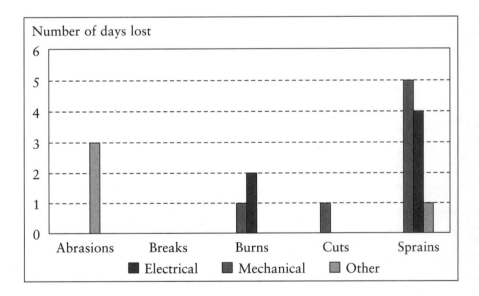

Figure 21.13. Lost work this month.

Root Cause Analysis

Root cause is the most basic reason for an undesirable effect (condition or problem), which if eliminated or corrected would have prevented the effect from existing or occurring. Root cause has three primary characteristics.

- It causes the effect—either directly, or through a sequence of intermediate causes and effects.

- It is controllable—intervention would change that cause.

- Its elimination will result in the elimination or reduction of the effect.[43]

Root cause analysis refers to the process of identifying causal factors. It can be an informal or structured approach. Care must be taken to distinguish symptoms clearly from causes, as well as apparent causes from root causes. Symptoms are the tangible evidence or manifestations indicating the existence or occurrence of a problem. Apparent causes represent the immediate or obvious reason for a problem.[44] The root cause must be corrected to prevent the problem from recurring.

Many methods are available for analyzing data to ultimately determine the root cause. Less structured techniques include flowcharts, process control charts, trend analysis, Pareto diagrams, nominal group techniques, and brainstorming. More formal root cause analysis techniques include barrier analysis, change analysis, event and causal factors analysis, tree diagrams, and cause-and-effect diagrams.

DESCRIPTIVE STATISTICS

"Descriptive statistics furnish a simple method of extracting information from what often seems at first glance to be a mass of random numbers. These characteristics of the data may relate to:

1. Typical, or central, value (mean, median, mode)

2. A measure of how much variability is present (variance, standard deviation)

3. A measure of frequency (percentiles)"[45]

Statistics is concerned with scientific methods for collecting, organizing, summarizing, presenting, and analyzing data, as well as drawing valid conclusions and making reasonable decisions on the basis of such analysis. In a narrower sense, the term *statistics* is used to denote the data themselves or numbers derived from the data, such as averages.[46]

An auditor must look at how an auditee defines the process and necessary controls, and establish some type of measurement system to ensure that the measurements or the process definitions were properly defined. The auditor looks at the results of what other people have done and, if they use these tools, must be knowledgeable enough to decide if the information that they are gathering from the data is valid. The phase of statistics that seeks only to describe and analyze a given group (sample) without drawing any conclusions or inferences about a larger group (population) is referred to as deductive or descriptive statistics. Measures of central tendency and dispersion are the two most fundamental concepts in statistical analysis.

Measures of Central Tendency

"Most frequency distributions exhibit a 'central tendency' (a shape such that the bulk of the observations pile up in the area between the two extremes)."[47] Central tendency is one of the most fundamental concepts in all statistical analysis. There are three principal measures of central tendency.

Arithmetic Mean. The arithmetic mean, or mean value, is the sum total of all data values divided by the number of data values. It is the simple arithmetic average of the total of the sample values. Mean is the most commonly used measure of central tendency and is the only such measure that includes every value in the data set. The arithmetic mean is used for symmetrical or near symmetrical distributions, or for distributions that lack a single clearly dominant peak.

Median. The median is the middle value (midpoint) of a data set arranged in numerical order, either in ascending or descending order. The median is used for reducing the effects of extreme values, or for data that can be ranked but are not economically measurable, such as shades of colors, odors, appearances, and the like.

Mode. The mode is the value or number that occurs most frequently in a data set. If all of the values are different, no mode exists. If two values have the most and same frequency of occurrence, then the data set or distribution has two modes and is referred to as *bimodal.* The mode is used for severely skewed distributions, for describing an irregular situation when two peaks are found, or for eliminating the observed effects of extreme values.

Measures of Dispersion

Dispersion is the variation in the spread of data about the mean. Dispersion is also referred to as variation, spread, and scatter. A measure of dispersion is the second of the two most fundamental measures of all statistical analyses. The dispersion within a central tendency is normally measured by one or more of several measuring principles.

Data are always scattered around the zone of central tendency, and the extent of this scatter is called dispersion or variation. There are several measures of dispersion.

Range. The range is the simplest measure of dispersion. Range is the difference between the maximum and minimum values in an observed data set. Since it is based on only two values from a data set, the measurement of range is most useful when the number of observations or values is small (10 or fewer).

Standard Deviation. Standard deviation, the most important measure of variation, measures the extent of dispersion around the zone of central tendency. For samples from a normal distribution, it is defined as the resulting value of the square root of the sum of the squares of the observed values, minus the arithmetic mean (numerator), divided by the total number of observations minus one (denominator).

Coefficient of Variation. Coefficient of variation is the final measure of dispersion, the standard deviation divided by the mean. Variance is the guaranteed existence of a difference between any two items or observations. The concept of variation states that no two observed items will ever be identical.

Appendix
CQA Body of Knowledge*

The following is an outline of the topics that constitute the Body of Knowledge for Quality Auditing.

I. **General Knowledge, Conduct, Ethics, Audit Administration— 45 Questions**
    A. General Knowledge
        1. Characteristics of audits
            a. Quality audits
            b. System, process, product, compliance audits
            c. Internal and external audits
            d. First party, second party, and third party audits
            e. Qualitative and quantitative audit methods
            f. Objective evidence
        2. Use of standard ASQC auditing terms and definitions
        3. Benefits of audits
        4. Continuing education resources for auditors
        5. Changes and trends in auditing practice

*Reprinted from ASQC Certification Department, *Certified Quality Auditor* booklet (Milwaukee: ASQC, 1996), pp. 12–14.

B. Professional Conduct and Ethics
   1. ASQC Code of Ethics
   2. Standards of performance for an auditor
      a. Appropriate auditor behavior
   3. Confidentiality concerns throughout audit process
   4. Auditor's responsibilities
      a. In unethical activities
      b. In unsafe activities
      c. Audit-related conflict of interest situations
   5. Methods for resolving difficult situations (e.g., antagonism)
   6. Language when communicating with management
C. Audit Administration
   1. Audit program objectives
   2. Methods for building credibility of audit function
   3. Management of the audit function

II. **Audit Preparation—30 Questions**
A. Audit Plan Preparation and Documentation
   1. Purpose
   2. Scope
   3. Resources
B. Audit Team Selection Criteria
   1. Credentials
   2. Expertise (skill and knowledge)
   3. Accountability
C. Sources of Authority for Conducting Audits
   1. Standards
      a. Industry
      b. National/International
   2. Organization
   3. Hierarchy
   4. Contract
   5. Regulatory

    D. Requirements Against Which to Audit
      1. Standards
      2. Contract
      3. Specifications
      4. Policy
    E. Importance and Utility of Quality Documentation
      1. Appropriate
      2. Adequate
      3. Accurate
      4. Current
      5. Prior audit information
    F. Checklists/Guidelines/Log Sheets
      1. Tailored for specific audit
      2. Update existing documents
      3. Appropriate use (nonlimiting)
    G. Development of Data Collection Method(s)
      1. Selecting appropriate tools
      2. Training the auditor in its use
      3. Criteria for selecting the methods
    H. Audit Plan Communication and Distribution

III. Audit Performance—30 Questions
    A. Conducting the Opening/Entrance Meeting
      1. Agenda
        a. Purpose
        b. Objectives
        c. Scope
        d. Logistics
        e. Standards
        f. Schedule
      2. Working papers
      3. Responsibilities and roles
      4. Attendees (who should be there)

B. Audit Team Management
  1. General auditing strategies
     a. Tracing forward/backward
     b. Discovery
     c. Department method
     d. Element method
  2. Management of the audit team
C. Audit Implementation
  1. Interviewing/questioning techniques
     a. Individual
     b. Group
     c. Telephone
     d. Remote
  2. Purposes and uses of data collection method(s)
     a. Analysis
     b. Detection
     c. Summary
     d. Verification
     e. Presentation
  3. Methods for verifying documents and records
     a. Tracing
     b. Sampling
     c. Physical examination
  4. Calibration principles and practices
     a. Traceability to recognize international/national standards
D. Audit Analysis
  1. Distinction between chronic and isolated incidents
  2. Classification of nonconformances and noncompliances
  3. Measures for determining effectiveness of controls
E. Closing/Exit Meeting
  1. Elements of closing meeting

IV. **Audit Reporting, Corrective Action, Follow-Up, and Closure—
25 Questions**
A. Reporting
  1. Format and contents of a formal audit report
     a. Identify auditee, client, purpose, and scope of audit

       b. Identify audit team members

       c. Identify standard(s) audit was performed to

       d. Significant observations and conclusions

       e. Request/requirements for corrective actions

       f. Distribution of report

    2. Techniques for prioritizing significant observations and conclusions

       a. Pareto analysis

       b. Risk benefit ratio

       c. Criticality

    3. Recognition of potential effects for similar conditions elsewhere in system/organization

B. Corrective Action and Follow-Up

    1. Types of corrective action

       a. Short term/temporary/containment

       b. Long term/permanent/root cause

    2. Criteria for acceptable corrective action

       a. Timely

       b. Effectiveness

       c. Preventive

    3. Strategies for verifying corrective actions

       a. Check action vs. standard

       b. Review of quality data

       c. Documentation evaluation

       d. Follow-up visit/audit

    4. Relationship between auditing function and continuous improvement

C. Closure

    1. Criteria for closure

       a. Time period

       b. Corrective action received, accepted, verified

       c. Retention of pertinent paperwork

       d. Notice to auditee indicating closure

    2. Criteria for record retention

V. **Auditing Tools and Techniques—25 Questions**
   A. Auditing Techniques
      1. Observation techniques
      2. Physical examination tools and techniques
      3. Presentation methods and techniques
      4. Time management techniques
      5. Sampling theory, procedures, applications for auditing
   B. Auditing Tools
      1. Definition and use of charts
         a. Flowcharts/process maps
         b. Pareto charts
         c. Cause-and-effect diagrams
         d. Control/trend charting
            (1) Variable
            (2) Attribute
      2. Graphs
         a. Histograms
         b. Frequency distributions
            (1) Definition
            (2) Types
         c. Process capability
      3. Pattern and trend analysis
      4. Root cause analysis
      5. Descriptive statistics
         a. Central tendency (mean, median, mode)
         b. Standard deviation
         c. Variable and attribute data

References

Chapter 1

1. Dennis R. Arter, *Quality Audits for Improved Performance,* 2d ed. (Milwaukee: ASQC Quality Press, 1994), p. 1.

2. Charles A. Mills, *The Quality Audit: A Management Evaluation Tool* (New York: McGraw-Hill, 1989), pp. 2–3. Reproduced with permission of The McGraw-Hill Companies.

3. ASQC Certification Department, "ASQC Certified Quality Auditor" brochure (Milwaukee: ASQC, 1996).

4. ANSI/ISO/ASQC A8402-1994, *Quality Management and Quality Assurance—Vocabulary* (Milwaukee: ASQC, 1994), p. 8.

5. Arter, p. 4.

6. Mills, p. 11.

7. ANSI/ISO/ASQC A8402-1994, p. 5.

8. Ibid.

9. Mills, pp. 5, 6, 7.

10. Allan J. Sayle, *Management Audits: The Assessment of Quality Management Systems,* 2d ed., ISBN 0-9511739-1-X (Great Britain: Allan J. Sayle Associates, 1988), pp. 1–7. Reproduced with permission of Allan J. Sayle.

11. Walter Willborn, *Audit Standards: A Comparative Analysis,* 2d ed. (Milwaukee: ASQC Quality Press, 1993), p. 31.

12. Arter, p. 4.

13. B. Scott Parsowith, *Fundamentals of Quality Auditing* (Milwaukee: ASQC Quality Press, 1995), pp. 4–5.

14. Shyam Banik, "Auditing," unpublished paper, p. 3.

15. Mills, p. 31.

16. Banik, p. 3.

17. Arter, p. 13.

18. ASQC Energy Division, *Nuclear Quality Systems Auditor Training Handbook,* 2d ed. (Milwaukee: ASQC Quality Press, 1986), p. 3.

19. ASQC Certification Department.

20. ASQC Energy Division, p. 2.

21. ASQC Certification Department.

22. Ibid.

23. ANSI/ISO/ASQC A8402-1994, p. 4.

24. Arter, pp. 1–2.

25. Arter, p. 3.

26. ANSI/ISO/ASQC A8402-1994, p. 5.

27. Willborn, pp. 52–53.

28. Allan J. Sayle, *Management Audits: The Assessment of Quality Management Systems,* 2d ed., ISBN 0-9511739-1-X (Great Britain: Allan J. Sayle Associates, 1988), pp. 1–4. Reproduced with permission of Allan J. Sayle.

29. J. M. Juran and Frank M. Gryna, eds., *Juran's Quality Control Handbook,* 4th ed. (New York: McGraw-Hill, 1988), p. 9.4. Reproduced with permission of The McGraw-Hill Companies.

30. Mills, p. 26.

31. American Productivity and Quality Center, "What Is Benchmarking" brochure (APQC, 123 North Post Oak Lane, 3rd Floor, Houston, TX 77024-7797).

32. J. P. Russell and Terry Regel, *After the Quality Audit: Closing the Loop on the Audit Process* (Milwaukee: ASQC Quality Press, 1996), pp. 157–167.

33. Charles B. Robinson, *How to Make the Most the Every Audit: An Etiquette Handbook for Auditing* (Milwaukee: ASQC Quality Press, 1992), p. 12.

34. Glena Anger et al., "Audit Ethics," unpublished paper, p. 15.

Chapter 2

1. Anger et al., p. 1.

2. ASQC Certification Department.

3. Mills, p. 87.

4. Anger et al., p. 2.

5. Ibid.

6. Willborn, p. 15.

7. Ibid., p. 22.

8. Anger et al., p. 4.

9. Ibid., pp. 8–9.

10. Ibid., p. 8.

11. L. F. MacArthur, "Audits and Liability Considerations," unpublished paper, p. 2.

12. Anger et al., p. 7.

13. ANSI/ISO/ASQC Q10011-2-1994, *Guidelines for Auditing Quality Systems* (Milwaukee: ASQC, 1994), p. 10, clause 10.0.

14. Anger et al., p. 5.

15. Anger et al., pp. 6–7.

Chapter 3

1. ASQC Certification Department.
2. Arter, pp. 5–6.
3. Robinson, *How to Make the Most of Every Audit,* p. 78.
4. Arter, p. 9.
5. Allan J. Sayle, *Management Audits: The Assessment of Quality Management Systems,* 2d ed., ISBN 0-9511739-1-X (Great Britain: Allan J. Sayle Associates, 1988), pp. 1–8. Reproduced with permission of Allan J. Sayle.
6. Parsowith, p. 14.
7. Anger et al., p. 10.

Chapter 4

1. Arter, p. 10.
2. Ibid., p. 12.
3. Willborn, p. 45.

Chapter 5

1. ASQC Energy Division, p. 26.
2. Ibid.
3. Ibid., p. 40.
4. Ibid., p. 25.
5. Willborn, p. 13.
6. Ibid.
7. Ibid., p. 14.
8. Ibid., p. 15.

Chapter 6

1. Arter, p. 18.

Chapter 7

1. Juran and Gryna, p. 9.6.
2. Arter, pp. 19–20.
3. Mills, p. 89.
4. Mills, p. 8.

Chapter 8

1. Arter, p. 35.

Chapter 9

1. Joseph H. Maday Jr., "The Audit Checklist: Your Key to Success," unpublished paper, p. 1.
2. Ibid., p. 2.
3. ASQC Energy Division, p. 26.
4. Ibid.

Chapter 10

1. Arter, pp. 32–33.

Chapter 11

1. Arter, p. 23.
2. Ibid., p. 26.

Chapter 12

1. Arter, p. 37.
2. ASQC Energy Division, p. 42.
3. Ibid.
4. Mills, p. 185.

Chapter 13

1. Parsowith, p. 24.

2. Arter, p. 41.

3. Parsowith, p. 23.

4. Kathryn E. Jackson and Thomas B. Tucker, "Meetings: Keeping Lines of Communication Open," unpublished paper, p. 2.

Chapter 14

1. Arter, pp. 39–40.

2. Kathryn E. Jackson and Thomas B. Tucker, "Gathering Data Through Employee and Customer Interviews," unpublished paper, p. 1.

3. Arter, p. 43.

4. Jackson and Tucker, "Gathering . . . ," p. 1.

5. Arter, p. 42.

6. "The Standards Scene," *The Standard: The Newsletter of the Measurement Quality Division* (Spring 1996), p. 15.

7. Dorsey J. Talley, *Management Audits for Excellence* (Milwaukee: ASQC Quality Press, 1988), p. 42.

8. Parsowith, pp. 52–53.

9. Ibid., p. 53.

Chapter 15

1. Arter, pp. 57–58.

2. Jackson and Tucker, "Meetings . . . ," p. 4.

Chapter 16

1. ASQC Energy Division, p. 45.

2. Parsowith, p. 30.

3. Arter, p. 62.

Chapter 17

1. Willborn, pp. 57, 34, 58.

2. ASQC Energy Division, p. 47.

3. Arter, p. 69.

Chapter 18

1. Charles B. Robinson, *Auditing a Quality System for the Defense Industry* (Milwaukee: ASQC Quality Press, 1990), p. 66.

2. Arter, p. 73.

3. ASQC Energy Division, p. 49.

4. Robinson, *Auditing a Quality System for the Defense Industry*, p. 66.

Chapter 19

1. Parsowith, p. 32.

2. Willborn, p. 65.

3. Parsowith, p. 33.

4. ASQC Energy Division, p. 32.

5. Arter, p. 78.

6. Ibid.

7. Ibid.

8. ASQC Energy Division, p. 34.

Chapter 20

1. Parsowith, pp. 7–8.

Chapter 21

1. Jerry Nation, "Auditing Tools," unpublished paper, p. 2.

2. Ibid., p. 3.

3. Ibid.

4. Ibid., p. 5.

5. Ibid., p. 6.

6. Ibid.

7. Ibid.

8. Ibid.

9. Ibid.

10. Ibid.

11. John T. Burr, "The Tools of Quality, Part I: Going with the Flow(chart)," *Quality Progress* (June 1990), p. 64.

12. Nation, p. 7.

13. Rudolph C. Hirzel, "Audits Making a Difference" (presented at the ASQC Fifth Annual Quality Audit Conference, 22-23 February 1996, Kansas City, Missouri).

14. Dianne Galloway, *Mapping Work Processes* (Milwaukee: ASQC Quality Press, 1994), p. 1.

15. Rudolph C. Hirzel, "Audits Making a Difference" (presented at the ASQC Fifth Annual Quality Audit Conference, 22–23 February 1996, Kansas City, Missouri).

16. Hirzel.

17. John T. Burr, "The Tools of Quality, Part VI: Pareto Charts," *Quality Progress* (November 1990), p. 61.

18. J. Stephen Sarazen (President, EXL Group, Andover, Mass.), "The Tools of Quality, Part II: Cause-and-Effect Diagrams," *Quality Progress* (July 1990), p. 59.

19. Ibid., p. 59.

20. Hirzel.

21. Ibid.

22. Nation, p. 12.

23. Juran Institute, "The Tools of Quality, Part IV: Histograms,

Quality Progress (September 1990), p. 76. This material is an excerpt from Juran Institute's publication, *Quality Improvement Tools*.™ It is reproduced with permission from the copyright holder: Juran Institute, Inc., Wilton, Connecticut, 06897, USA.

24. Nation, p. 18.

25. Ibid., p. 20.

26. Ibid., p. 19.

27. Juran Institute, pp. 77–78.

28. Nation, p. 19.

29. Parsowith, p. xiii.

30. Peter D. Shainin, "The Tools of Quality, Part III: Control Charts," *Quality Progress* (August 1990), pp. 79, 80.

31. Nation, p. 13.

32. Juran and Gryna, p. 24.8.

33. Ibid., p. 24.7.

34. Parsowith, p. 65.

35. Juran and Gryna, p. 22.41.

36. Nation, p. 21.

37. Mills, p. 205.

38. Ibid., p. 214.

39. Hirzel.

40. Ibid.

41. Ibid.

42. Ibid.

43. Nation, p. 24.

44. Ibid., p. 25.

45. Juran and Gryna, p. 23.15.

46. Nation, p. 25.

47. Juran and Gryna, p. 23.16.

Glossary

Auditee Organization being audited

Business first party See *Contractor*

Business second party See *Purchaser*

Company-wide quality control (CWQC) See *Total quality management (TQM)*

Compatibility Ability of entities to be used together under specific conditions to fulfill relevant requirements

Concession Written authorization to use or release a product which does not conform to the specified requirements; see also *Waiver*

Contract review Systematic activities carried out by the supplier before signing the contract to ensure that requirements for quality are adequately defined, free from ambiguity, documented, and can be realized by the supplier

Contractor Supplier in a contractual situation

Correction Refers to repair, rework, or adjustment and relates to the disposition of an existing nonconformity

*ANSI/ISO/ASQC A8402-1994, *Quality Management and Quality Assurance—Vocabulary* (Milwaukee: ASQC, 1994). Reprinted with permission.

Corrective action Action taken to eliminate the causes of an existing nonconformity, defect, or other undesirable situation in order to prevent recurrence

Customer Recipient of a product provided by the supplier

Defect Nonfulfillment of an intended usage requirement or reasonable expectation, including one concerned with safety

Degree of demonstration Extent to which evidence is produced to provide confidence that specified requirements are fulfilled

Dependability Collective term used to describe the availability performance and its influencing factors: reliability performance, maintainability performance, and maintenance-support performance

Design review Documented, comprehensive, and systematic examination of a design to evaluate its capability to fulfill the requirements for quality, identify problems, if any, and propose the development of solutions

Deviation permit Written authorization to depart from the originally specified requirements for a product prior to its production; see also *Production permit*

Disposition of nonconformity Action to be taken to deal with an existing nonconforming entity in order to resolve the nonconformity

Entity Item which can be individually described and considered

Grade Category or rank given to entities having the same functional use but different requirements for quality

Hold point Point, defined in an appropriate document, beyond which an activity must not proceed without the approval of a designated organization or authority

Inspection Activity such as measuring, examining, testing, or gauging one or more characteristics of an entity and comparing the results with specified requirements in order to establish whether conformity is achieved for each characteristic

Interchangeability Ability of an entity to be used in place of another, without modification, to fulfill the same requirements

Item See *Entity*

Lead quality auditor A quality auditor designated to manage a quality audit

Management review Formal evaluation by top management of the status and adequacy of the quality system in relation to quality policy and objectives

Model for quality assurance Standardized or selected set of quality system requirements combined to satisfy the quality assurance needs of a given situation

Nonconformity Nonfulfillment of a specified requirement

Objective evidence Information which can be proved true, based on facts obtained through observation, measurement, test, or other means

Organization Company, corporation, firm, enterprise, or institution, or part thereof, whether incorporated or not, public or private, that has its own functions and administration

Organizational structure Responsibilities, authorities, and relationships, arranged in a pattern, through which an organization performs its functions

Preventive action Action taken to eliminate the causes of a potential nonconformity, defect, or other undesirable situation in order to prevent occurrence

Procedure Specified way to perform an activity

Process Set of interrelated resources and activities which transform inputs into outputs

Process quality audit See *Quality audit*

Process quality evaluation See *Quality evaluation*

Product Results on activities or processes

Product liability Generic term used to describe the onus on a producer or others to make restitution for loss related to personal injury, property damage, or other harm caused by a product

Product quality audit See *Quality audit*

Production permit See *Deviation permit*. A production permit is for a limited quantity or period and for a specified use

Purchaser Customer in a contractual situation

Qualification See *Qualification process*

Qualification process Process of demonstrating whether an entity is capable of fulfilling the specified requirement

Qualified Status given to an entity when the capability of fulfilling specified requirements has been demonstrated

Quality Totality of characteristics of an entity that bear on its ability to satisfy stated and implied needs

Quality appraisal See *Quality evaluation*

Quality assessment See *Quality evaluation*

Quality assurance All the planned and systematic activities implemented within the quality system, and demonstrated as needed, to provide adequate confidence that an entity will fulfill requirements for quality

Quality assurance manual See *Quality manual*

Quality assurance plan See *Quality plan*

Quality audit Systematic and independent examination to determine whether quality activities and related results comply with planned arrangements and whether these arrangements are implemented effectively and are suitable to achieve objectives

Quality audit observation Statement of fact made during a quality audit and substantiated by objective evidence

Quality auditor Person qualified to perform quality audits

Quality control Operational techniques and activities that are used to fulfill requirements for quality

Quality evaluation Systematic examination of the extent to which an entity is capable of fulfilling specified requirements

Quality improvement Actions taken throughout the organization to increase the effectiveness and efficiency of activities and processes in order to provide added benefits to both the organization and its customers

Quality loop Conceptual model of interacting activities that influence quality at the various stages ranging from the identification of needs to the assessment of whether these needs have been satisfied

Quality losses Losses caused by not realizing the potential of resources in processes and activities

Quality management All activities of the overall management function that determine the quality policy, objectives, and responsibilities, and implement them by means such as quality planning, quality control, quality assurance, and quality improvement within the quality system

Quality management manual See *Quality manual*

Quality management plan See *Quality plan*

Quality manual Document stating the quality policy and describing the quality system of an organization

Quality plan Document setting out the specific quality practices, resources, and sequence of activities relevant to a particular product, project, or contract

Quality planning Activities that establish the objectives and requirements for quality and for the application of quality system elements

Quality policy Overall intentions and direction of an organization with regard to quality, as formally expressed by top management

Quality record Document which provides objective evidence of the extent of the fulfillment of the requirements for quality or the effectiveness of the operation of a quality system element

Quality-related costs Those costs incurred in ensuring and assuring satisfactory quality, as well as the losses incurred when satisfactory quality is not achieved

Quality spiral See *Quality loop*

Quality surveillance Continual monitoring and verification of the status of an entity and analysis of records to ensure that specified requirements are being fulfilled

Quality survey See *Quality evaluation*

Quality system Organizational structure, procedures, processes, and resources needed to implement quality management

Quality system record See *Quality record*

Record Document which furnishes objective evidence of activities performed or results achieved

Repair Action taken on a nonconforming product so that it will fulfill the intended usage requirements although it may not conform to the originally specified requirements

Requirements for quality Expression of the needs or their translation into a set of quantitatively or qualitatively stated requirements for the characteristics of an entity to enable its realization and examination

Requirements of society Obligations resulting from laws, regulations, rules, codes, statutes, and other considerations

Rework Action taken on a nonconforming product so that it will fulfill the specified requirements

Safety State in which the risk of harm (to persons) or damage is limited to an acceptable level

Self-inspection Inspection of the work by the performer of that work, according to specified rules

Service Result generated by activities at the interface between the supplier and the customer and by supplier internal activities to meet the customer needs

Service delivery Those supplier activities necessary to provide the service

Service quality audit See *Quality audit*

Specification Document stating requirements

Subcontractor Organization that provides a product to the supplier

Subsupplier See *Subcontractor*

Supplier Organization that provides a product to the customer

Total quality See *Total quality management (TQM)*

Total quality control (TQC) See *Total quality management (TQM)*

Total quality management (TQM) Management approach of an organization, centered on quality, based on the participation of all its members and aiming at long-term success through customer satisfaction, and benefits to all members of the organization and to society

Traceability Ability to trace the history, application, or location of an entity by means of recorded identifications

Validation Confirmation by examination and provision of objective evidence that the particular requirements for a specified intended use are fulfilled

Verification Confirmation by examination and provision of objective evidence that specified requirements have been fulfilled

Waiver See *Concession*. A waiver is limited to the shipment of a product that has specific nonconforming characteristics within specific deviations, for a limited time or quantity

DEFINITIONS TAKEN FROM ASQC CQA BROCHURE

Assessment An estimate or determination of the significance, importance, or value of something.

Audit A planned, independent, and documented assessment to determine whether agreed-upon requirements are being met.

Audit program The organizational structure, commitment, and documented methods used to plan and perform audits.

Audit standard The authentic description of essential characteristics of audits that reflects current thought and practice.

Audit team The group of individuals conducting an audit under the direction of a team leader. relevant to a particular product, process, service, contract, or project.

Auditee An organization to be audited.

Auditing organization A unit or function that carries out audits through its employees. This organization may be a department of the auditee, a client, or an independent third party.

Auditor The individual who carries out the audit.

Certification The procedure and action, by a duly authorized body, of determining, verifying, and attesting in writing to the qualifications of personnel, processes, procedures, or items in accordance with applicable requirements.

Characteristic A property that helps to identify or to differentiate between entities and that can be described or measured to determine conformance or nonconformance to requirements.

Client The person or organization requesting the audit. Depending on the circumstances, the client may be the auditing organization, the auditee, or a third party.

Compliance An affirmative indication or judgment that the supplier of a product or service has met the requirements of the relevant specifications, contract, or regulation; also the state of meeting the requirements.

Conformance An affirmative indication or judgment that a product or service has met the requirements of the relevant specifications, contract, or regulation; also the state of meeting the requirements.

Contractor Any organization under contract to furnish items or services: a vendor, supplier, subcontractor, fabricator, and sub-tier levels of these, where appropriate.

Convention A customary practice, rule, or method.

Corrective action Action taken to eliminate the root cause(s) and symptom(s) of an existing undesirable deviation or nonconformity to prevent recurrence.

Deviation A nonconformance or departure of a characteristic from specified product, process, or systems requirements.

Finding A conclusion of importance based on observation(s).

Follow-up audit An audit whose purpose and scope are limited to verifying that corrective action has been accomplished as scheduled and to determining that the action prevented recurrence effectively.

Guidelines Documented instructions that are considered good practice but that are not mandatory.

Independence Freedom from bias and external influences.

Inspection Activities—such as measuring, examining, and testing—that gauge one or more characteristics of a product or service and the comparison of these with specified requirements to determine conformity.

Objective evidence Verifiable qualitative or quantitative observations, information, records, or statements of fact pertaining to the quality of an item or service or to the existence and implementation of a quality system element.

Observation An item of objective evidence found during an audit.

Procedure A document that specifies the way to perform an activity.

Process quality audit An analysis of elements of a process and appraisal of completeness, correctness of conditions, and probable effectiveness.

Product quality audit A quantitative assessment of conformance to required product characteristics.

Qualification The status given to an entity or person when the fulfillment of specified requirements has been demonstrated; the process of obtaining that status.

Quality assurance All those planned and systematic actions necessary to provide adequate confidence that a product or service will satisfy given quality requirements.

Quality audit A systematic and independent examination and evaluation to determine whether quality activities and results comply with planned arrangements and whether these arrangements are implemented effectively and are suitable to achieving objectives.

Quality control The operational techniques and activities that are used to fulfill requirements for quality.

Quality manual A document stating the quality policy, quality system, and quality practices of an organization.

Quality plan A document setting out the specific quality practices, resources, and activities relevant to a particular product, process, service, contract, or project.

Quality policy The overall intentions and direction of an organization regarding quality, as formally expressed by top management.

Quality surveillance The continuing monitoring and verification of the status of procedures, methods, conditions, products, processes, and services and the analysis of records in relation to stated references to ensure that requirements for quality are being met.

Quality system The organizational structure, responsibilities, procedures, processes, and resources for implementing quality management.

Quality system audit A documented activity performed to verify, by examination and evaluation of objective evidence, that applicable elements of the quality system are suitable and have been developed, documented, and effectively implemented in accordance with specified requirements.

Quality system review A formal evaluation by management of the status and adequacy of the quality system in relation to quality policy and/or new objectives resulting from changing circumstances.

Root cause A fundamental deficiency that results in a nonconformance and must be corrected to prevent recurrence of the same or similar nonconformance.

Specification The document that prescribes the requirements to which the product or service must conform.

Standard The documented result of a particular standardization effort approved by a recognized authority.

Survey An examination for some specific purpose; to inspect or consider carefully; to review in detail. (Note: some authorities use the words *audit* and *survey* interchangeably. *Audit* implies the existence of some agreed-upon criteria against which the plans and execution can be checked. *Survey* implies the inclusion of matters not covered by agreed-upon criteria.)

Testing A means of determining an item's capability to meet specified requirements by subjecting the item to a set of physical, chemical, environmental, or operating actions and conditions.

Traceability The ability to trace the history, application, or location of an item or activity and like items or activities by means of recorded identification.

Verification The act of reviewing, inspecting, testing, checking, auditing, or otherwise establishing and documenting whether items, processes, services, or documents conform to specified requirements.

Bibliography

American Productivity and Quality Center. "What Is Benchmarking" brochure. Houston, Tex.: APQC.

ANSI/ISO/ASQC A8402-1994. *Quality Management and Quality Assurance—Vocabulary*. Milwaukee: ASQC, 1994.

ANSI/ISO/ASQC Q10011-2-1994. *Guidelines for Auditing Quality Systems*. Milwaukee: ASQC, 1994.

Arter, Dennis R. *Quality Audits for Improved Performance*. 2d ed. Milwaukee: ASQC Quality Press, 1994.

ASQC Energy Division. *Nuclear Quality Systems Auditor Training Handbook*. 2d ed. Milwaukee: ASQC Quality Press, 1986.

Burr, John T. "The Tools of Quality, Part I: Going with the Flow(chart)." *Quality Progress* (June 1990), p. 64.

———. "The Tools of Quality, Part VI: Pareto Charts. *Quality Progress* (November 1990), p. 61.

Galloway, Dianne. *Mapping Work Processes*. Milwaukee: ASQC Quality Press, 1994.

Juran, J. M., ed. *Juran's Quality Control Handbook*. 4th ed. New York: McGraw-Hill, 1988.

Juran Institute. "The Tools of Quality, Part IV: Histograms." *Quality Progress* (September 1990), p. 76.

Mills, Charles A. *The Quality Audit: A Management Evaluation Tool.* New York: McGraw-Hill, 1989.

Parsowith, B. Scott. *Fundamentals of Quality Auditing.* Milwaukee: ASQC Quality Press, 1995.

Robinson, Charles B. *Auditing a Quality System for the Defense Industry.* Milwaukee: ASQC Quality Press, 1990.

Robinson, Charles B. *How to Make the Most of Every Audit: An Etiquette Handbook for Auditing.* Milwaukee: ASQC Quality Press, 1992.

Russell, J. P., and Terry Regel. *After the Quality Audit: Closing the Loop on the Audit Process.* Milwaukee: ASQC Quality Press, 1996.

Sarazen, J. Stephen. "The Tools of Quality, Part II: Cause-and-Effect Diagrams." *Quality Progress* (July 1990), p. 59.

Sayle, Allan J. *Management Audits: The Assessment of Quality Management Systems.* 2d ed. Great Britain: Allan J. Sayle, 1988.

Shainin, Peter D. "The Tools of Quality, Part III: Control Charts." *Quality Progress* (August 1990), pp. 79–80.

"The Standards Scene." *The Standard: The Newsletter of the Measurement Quality Division* (spring 1996), p. 15.

Talley, Dorsey J. *Management Audits for Excellence.* Milwaukee: ASQC Quality Press, 1988.

Willborn, Walter. *Audit Standards: A Comparative Analysis.* 2d ed. Milwaukee: ASQC Quality Press, 1993.

Index